QUEEN ELIZABETH.
ENGLAND'S MOST ILLUSTRIOUS SOVEREIGN.

A Thousand Years With Royalty

A Story of the English Kings

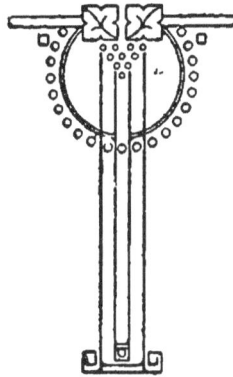

By J. McN. JOHNSON

Notice

In many older books, foxing (or discoloration) occurs and, in some instances, print lightens with wear and age. Reprinted books, such as this, often duplicate these flaws, notwithstanding efforts to reduce or eliminate them. The pages of this reprint have been digitally enhanced and, where possible, the flaws eliminated in order to provide clarity of content and a pleasant reading experience.

To my young son
Felix Leslie Johnson,
whose early literary bent,
as evidenced by incessant and
innumerable questions, forced me
to become, superficially,
conversant with English history,
I dedicate this simple
compilation.

PREFACE

I remember once when a boy, I asked the late James Davis, an old-time schoolmaster, why it was that an author wrote a preface to his book? His answer was that usually the poor man discovered that the book needed an apology.

This simple compilation is admittedly without intrinsic merit. It had its inception in notes that I had taken some years ago, when assisting my own children in their history lessons. My idea at the time was to induce a personal interest in the king of the time the lesson referred to, and thus render less irksome the task directly in hand.

Who is it that does not know something of the barren desert that must be traversed before a single blossom of beauty is found in the field of history so rich in luscious browse after it is reached?

If I shall help some young and impressionable mind over this flowerless waste that has proven an impassable Sahara to so many bright young readers, I shall indeed be a fortunate man. If I fail in this particular, my effort will have proved an entire failure. But even then it is pleasant to think no real harm can have been done, for the labor has been a downright pleasure to me.

J. McN. Johnson.

Aberdeen, N. C.,
    August 1, 1913.

A Thousand Years With Royalty

A Story of the English Kings

It has been my purpose to write a story that may be read in a winter's night, embracing the forty-one sovereigns that have ruled in England since the Norman Conquest, and in their order of succession to give a short and concise description of each sovereign, such as would be likely to appeal to the minds of the young; but to round out my thousand years indicated in the caption above, it will be necessary for me to hark back about a century and a half—to be exact, one hundred and forty-six years before the Conquest—to find my starting point.

If it were possible for us to go back to England in the year A. D. 912, just a thousand years ago, we should find that King Alfred the Great had been dead eleven years, and that his son was king,

EDWARD THE ELDER.

This King's sovereignty extended only over the southern part of England, while all the northern part was under the control of the Danes.

In those days the English people were too often ruled in their actions by superstition, and King Edward the Elder was not greater nor wiser than his times. He had married a daughter of a peasant named Atheling, for the principal reason, it is said, that this young woman had had a dream that from her body there proceeded a great *Moon* that gave wondrous light to all England; and the people believed that this dream foretold that the dreamer should become the mother of great kings.

In due time the Wondrous Light appeared in the form of a little boy; and probably because of this prophetic dream, and because he was the grandson of the great Alfred, but more than all else, because he was directly related to the common people, he was idolized, fêted, and petted, and looked to as the Savior of England, while the king, though his reign was a prosperous one, found himself beholding his people waiting for the accession of the young prince with a complacency that must have aroused the jealousy of a less noble nature.

We know there was nothing in the dream; but it is sure that royalty gained one great advantage from this marriage, which was to endear the kings to their subjects; for we are told that for two hundred and fifty years, the common people, during a contest for the throne, invariably sided with the contestant that boasted the Atheling blood, and fondly called him "The Atheling."

Edward the Elder, after reigning twenty-four years, died in the year 925; for his reign began with the death of Alfred the Great in 901, and his son, the promised Wondrous Light, was crowned, as

ATHELSTANE.

This king, from the circumstance of his birth, as related above, was exceedingly popular, and under their trusted leader, the English people enjoyed a prestige and prosperity never before known. But after a reign of fifteen years, Athelstane died in the year 940, and was succeeded by his young brother,

6

EDMUND, The Atheling.

Edmund was the first of the Six Boy Kings. But, after a reign of six years, Edmund was murdered by an outlaw in his own banqueting hall, and was succeeded by his brother,

EDRED.

This was the second of the Six Boy Kings. This king, like all the other boy kings, was hopelessly dominated by Saint Dunstan, Abbot of Glastonbury, who, by the way, is not the only juggling rascal that has come to be called *Saint.* Edred reigned nine years, and died in the year 955, and was succeeded by his nephew, a young son of Edmund, as,

EDWY, The Fair.

So called because of his distinct Saxon features. This boy king's reign was of only three years' duration. He died in 958, and was succeeded by

EDGAR, The Peaceful.

This boy king was a brother of Edwy. While he was entirely dominated by Saint Dunstan and the other monks, we are told that he united the two kingdoms, Northumbria and Mercia, and during his whole reign there was no breath of war. Edgar reigned seventeen years, and died in the year 975, and was succeeded by his son,

EDWARD, The Martyr.

The reign of this king was terminated in 978, when Edward was treacherously murdered by order of his step-

7

mother, the wicked Elfrida. He was succeeded by his half-brother, a son of the murderess, whose name was

ETHELRED, The Unready.

It is said that the best thing this king did was to oust Saint Dunstan from authority; and his surname, Unready, was given him by Dunstan, in derision. The word had a somewhat different signification than that we now attach to it. We understand *Unready* to mean *not prepared*, or *not prompt*, but as applied to King Ethelred, it indicated that he was without an adviser, from the old Saxon word *rede*, advice. In other words, the king dispensed with the services of the Abbot of Glastonbury, and depended on his own judgment. For this we have only admiration; but in many ways this king was careless of the rights of his subjects, and Mr. Dickens says that when he died after thirty-nine years of misrule, he did as good a deed as he ever did in all his life.

King Ethelred depended largely on marriage alliances with his possible enemies, to insure a peaceful reign. He gave his sisters in marriage with the potentates of continental Europe, and himself married the princess Emma, a daughter of Duke Richard of Normandy; but the old enemy, the Dane, was not appeased, and was a constant menace to England during Ethelred's reign. This king died in the year 1016, and there was an immediate scramble for the throne, lest the Dane should seize upon it.

Ethelred's eldest son, hereafter to be known as Edward, The Confessor, was in banishment, and a younger son was proclaimed king, as,

8

EDMUND, IRONSIDES.

But the few months of this Edmund's reign was a bloody struggle with the Danes, and the shameless Emma, Edmund's own mother, turned against her son, and married the Danish contestant for the throne.

The importance of fixing the short reign of Edmund Ironsides in our minds lies in the fact that a great-granddaughter of Edmund Ironsides married Henry I., a Norman king, thus again grafting the blood of Alfred the Great, and also the blood of the Athelings, into the royal line of Norman kings.

After a compromise with the Danes, Edmund Ironsides reigned in London from April to November of the year 1016, and died, it is thought by the hand of a traitor named Edric, and the whole of England was immediately seized by the Danes, and ruled by that king known in history as,

CANUTE, THE DANE.

This was Emma's second husband, and lifelong enemy of Ethelred, her first husband. This Danish king tried hard to ingratiate himself with the English people, and ruled with more moderation than was to be expected from one of his wolfish nature; but the people could not forgive the unnatural Emma, and stood at arm's length with the Danish king.

Canute had an illegitimate son by a great, bold woman named Algiva of Northampton, and on the death of Canute in 1035, the Danes, with the assistance of those English who were willing to sacrifice nationality to punish Emma, forced this illegitimate son of Canute into the kingly office, as,

9

HAROLD, HAREFOOT.

This election excluded the sons of Emma by both her husbands, that is to say, Edward and Alfred, sons of Ethelred, and Hardi Canute, son of Canute. Harold Harefoot banished Emma, and this is the only creditable act of his reign. He treacherously invited Edward and Alfred, sons of Ethelred, to return from banishment; but Edward saw the snare, and prudently retired, while Alfred, suspecting no guile, accepted the invitation, and was ruthlessly murdered by the agents of Harold. Harold Harefoot died in 1040, and was succeeded by

HARDI CANUTE.

This king, half Dane and half Norman, but wholly Danish in his prejudices, was son of Canute and Emma; and it was a constant struggle during his short reign to uphold the anti-Saxon party. But now the Saxon tide had turned, and the Danish influence, as well as the influence of Emma, was on the wane. So on the death of Hardi Canute in 1043, the banished son of King Ethelred and this same Emma was recalled and crowned king of England, as,

EDWARD, THE CONFESSOR.

It has been said that Edward, on his accession to the throne, treated his unnatural mother with high disdain and scorn. But Edward the Confessor was a great and good king. For five hundred years after his death, when the English people petitioned against oppressive laws, they prayed that they be given back *"The Good Laws of Edward the Confessor."*

Edward the Confessor married a daughter of the great Earl Godwine, and, despite his religious life, which gained him the surname of Confessor, he has been accused of being unkind to this lady. Some historians believe this queen was *thrust* upon him by her father, for Godwine was as great and powerful in his day as was Warwick, the king-maker, during the Wars of the Roses.

This King Edward was a first cousin to William, Duke of Normandy, afterwards the Conqueror, and the Duke claimed that Edward had promised him the crown of England. But the king's brother-in-law, Harold, son of Earl Godwine, was the choice of the English people; and what with the influence of the people, and the queen, and Harold himself, Edward was persuaded against his own judgment, to name Harold as his successor. He knew very well there would be a struggle with the Normans, and was convinced in his own mind that the English could not successfully resist the Norman arms; but he was weak and sick, and finally yielded to the pressure.

Lord Tennyson, in his drama, "Harold," in language almost equal to Shakespeare's, depicts this struggle of the king, and gives us a clearer insight into the times than the historians give us. The oft-quoted lines, attributed to Edward by Tennyson, are taken from this drama:

"But heaven and earth are threads of the same loom,
Play into one another, and weave the web
That may confound thee yet."

Edward the Confessor died in January, 1066, and was succeeded by his brother-in-law,

HAROLD.

This king is known in history as, Last of the Saxon Kings, Earl of the West Saxons, and best and bravest of the sons of the Great Earl Godwine. But Harold reigned only nine months. In October of the same year, Duke William came over from Normandy with a great army, and, in the celebrated battle of Hastings, defeated the English under Harold, and Harold himself was slain by an arrow piercing his brain through his eye. The defeat of the English was turned into a rout, and William soon overran all England, putting down all opposition with an iron hand. This incident is known in history as The Norman Conquest. Duke William the Norman was crowned king of England on Christmas Day, 1066, as

WILLIAM I.

Better known as William the Conqueror, which he assumed as a surname. The blood of this man has flowed in the veins of every sovereign that has ruled in England since the battle of Hastings, with the single exception of Oliver Cromwell, the greatest ruler England ever saw.

This conquest was awful, cruel, and thorough. The Conqueror devastated vast areas of fertile grounds to make hunting parks. He burned thousands of English homes, and turned out homeless and to starve as many thousands of English women and children, to pleasure his whims. He conquered everything,—but the human heart. When he came to die not a single human being in all the world loved him! What a commentary on earthly greatness! Mr. Dickens refers to the Conqueror's end thus: "Think of his name, The Conqueror, and then consider how he lay in death! The moment he was dead, his physicians, priests and nobles, not knowing what contest for the throne might now take place, or what might happen in it, hastened away, each man for himself and his property; the mercenary servants of the court began to rob and plunder; the body of the king, in the indecent strife, was rolled from the bed and lay for hours on the ground. O Conqueror, of whom so many great names are proud now, of whom so many great names thought nothing then, it were better to have conquered one true heart than England!"

But a strong man is rarely a mean man, and cruel as was the conquest of the Norman, much good resulted to the English nation from this change of dynasties. The great Survey, the Domesday book, the new tenure of land-holding, and a better judicial system than England had ever known, largely compensated the nation, if not the individual, for the high-handed methods of the Conqueror in bringing the English people under the Norman yoke.

In the year 1087, William the Conqueror died, and was succeeded by his second son, who reigned over England as,

WILLIAM II.

This king was surnamed Rufus, which means red, and many historians call him the red king. He ruled with great harshness and extreme selfishness for thirteen years, and was killed by an arrow-shot in the "New Forest,"—that very forest taken from the common people by his father with such violence. It was never known certainly whether William II. was murdered, or accidentally shot by his companion in the chase, whose name was Tyrrell; but the common people firmly believed it to be an act of divine retribution.

It was during this reign that the first crusade occurred. Many of the greatest gentlemen in England marched to the Far East on this ill-advised enterprise, and never returned again; and on account of the harsh treatment of the Saxon nobles by the Normans, many of their young men left England and joined the Greek armies.

Sir Walter Scott's "Quentin Durward" gives us an interesting account both of the crusade and the emigration of the young Saxon nobles.

It was in the year 1100 William Rufus was killed, and as he died without issue, and his elder brother Robert was engaged in the crusade, he was succeeded by his younger brother, who virtually usurped the throne, and reigned as

HENRY I.

On account of Henry's proficiency in the learning of his time, the Normans had given him the surname of Beauclerk, which the English translated into *Fine Scholar.*

William the Conqueror, in his last will, bequeathed Normandy to his eldest son Robert, and England to William, while to Henry he gave the sum of five thousand pounds in money. This sum represented much greater wealth then than it does now, but it was so infinitely smaller than the portions given to Robert and William, privileged friends of the Conqueror, we are told, remonstrated against this treatment of the accomplished Henry; but the Conqueror knew his man. He knowingly replied: "Never mind, Henry will get it all in the end." And he did. When Henry I. died, he was king of England, and of Normandy, and had his five thousand pounds to boot.

There is a beautiful love story connected with this king, and its results have been far reaching in their consequences. You will recall that fifty-five years before the accession of Henry I. to the throne, we called attention to Edmund Ironsides, a Saxon king whose great-granddaughter married a Norman king. Now we have come to that king. Henry married Edith, a daughter of King Malcolm, of Scotland, and who was a novice in the convent at Romsey. Edith's mother was Margaret, a granddaughter of Edmund Ironsides.

We are told that Henry rode up to the convent gate at Romsey, and, seeing Edith the novice in all her beauty, asked her to be the queen of England. Edith's aunt was the Abbess of the convent, and used all her authority and powers of persuasion to induce Edith to refuse the offer; but to no purpose. Edith had not taken the vow, and the Archbishop Anselm absolved her from the vows other people had taken for her, and performed the marriage ceremony. Palgrave has written a beautiful little poem on this incident, one stanza of which follows:

"Then love smiled true on Henry's face,
    And Anselm joined the hands
That in one race two races bound,
    By everlasting bands.
So love is Lord, and Alfred's blood
    Returns the land to sway;
And all her joyous maidens join
    In their soft roundelay."

15

So it came about that Great Alfred's Saxon blood again flowed in the veins of English royalty, and the blended blood of Norman and Saxon became the dominating strain of the rulers of England.

Edith, on her marriage with Henry I., changed her name to Matilda, in compliment to Henry's mother. Her popularity was immense, and went far toward making the Britons forget that their king was an alien.

Henry I.'s eldest daughter, also named Matilda, married Jeffrey of Anjou, a fact I mention to show the line through which after-kings held the English crown.

This King Henry was much of the time at war with the states of continental Europe, and he was on one of these excursions when his beloved queen died. He returned saddened and almost heartbroken, and began to centre all his hopes in his young son William, whom the common people affectionately called *"The Atheling."* But now came the crowning sorrow. This son and his young sister were drowned when the *White Ship* struck on a rock and went to pieces while crossing the English Channel, engulfing all on board, with but a single survivor.

On hearing of this catastrophe, it is said Henry fell down in a swoon, and, though he lived many years thereafter, was never again known to smile.

On this tragedy Mrs. Hemans has written a touching poem, a stanza of which I here reproduce:

"The bark that held the prince went down,
　The sweeping waves rolled on,
And what was England's glorious crown
　To him that wept a son?
He lived, for life may long be borne
　Ere sorrow break its chain:
Why comes not death to those who mourne?
　He never smiled again."

After this tragedy Henry's only child was Matilda, the wife of Jeffrey of Anjou, and Henry attempted to settle the succession on her. England had never been ruled by a woman; indeed, the Salic Law, introduced into England by William, The Conqueror, declared that a woman was not capable of inheriting the crown, nor of transmitting the inheritance to her descendants, and Henry did not venture to order his subjects to do her reverence as a *queen*, but ordered that Matilda be recognized as "*Lady of England and Normandy*," by virtue of a sort of an amendment to the Salic Law, and this was done without question. Even Stephen, a son of Henry's sister, swore fealty to Matilda. So with his mind set at rest as to the succession, Henry I, in the year 1135, was gathered to his fathers; and Matilda came over to England to assume her dignities. To her astonishment the English people said, "Nay, Madam, England must be ruled by a king. The Salic Law is still in force." She was surrounded by her friends and partisans, but it was clear to see that a majority of the ruling class was bent on crowning that same Stephen that had sworn fealty to Matilda, and he was crowned king of England as,

STEPHEN, OF BLOIS.

Then for seventeen long years there was anarchy, and the nation was torn with civil war. Matilda was especially strong in Scotland, because her mother was a daughter of the Scottish king. She was also much beloved by the common people of England, who were determined that the blood of the Athelings should not again be expelled from the royal seat; while the ruling classes were as stubborn in their determination not to be ruled by a woman. (Poor, blinded creatures; every one of them was ruled by a woman at home!) At one time Matilda's forces actually captured Stephen, threw him into prison, and crowned Matilda; but this was for only a few days, and Matilda is not accounted a sovereign in the catalogue of English kings.

At last, in 1153, the Salic Law was so far abrogated as to allow a woman to transmit the inheritance of the crown, and a compromise was agreed upon, by the terms of which Stephen was to retain the crown during his natural life, but he should be succeeded by Matilda's son; an agreement that secured to each party all that was contended for, for Matilda's son was all that could be desired in manly and kingly bearing, and was a descendant of the Athelings, and of Alfred the Great.

The next year after the compromise, that is in the year 1154, Stephen died, and it appears that everybody was glad of it. With Stephen passed the line of Norman kings. He was succeeded by

HENRY II.

This king is known as Henry of Anjou, and was a grandson of Henry I. and Edith, the novice. He was the first of the line of Plantagenets.

The name *Plantagenet* signifies *Broom*, and was acquired by this great family during the wars of the crusades, when a leading warrior adopted a sprig of broom as his badge, so that he might be known by his own men during the confusion of battle. This warrior was bold and powerful, and his success in battle with the Turks gave him great popularity, and the war cry, *"Plante de genet"* became a synonym of victory; hence it was adopted as the surname of the warrior's family.

The royal sceptre remained with the house of Plantagenet through a line of fourteen kings, including three kings of the House of Lancaster and three of the House of York, ending with the death of Richard III. in 1485, of which we shall hear later in this history.

Henry II. was a tyrant, but tyranny is better than anarchy. Besides, he was of Saxon stock, and that made a great difference; for what might be intolerable tyranny of one man, might be almost unobjectionable, or even admirable, in some other man (so entirely are we ruled by prejudice); and because the English people had made up their minds to *like* their king, they greatly prospered under Henry II.

Henry inherited large domains on the continent: to these he added still larger by his marriage with Eleanor, the divorced wife of Louis the Young. So, when he came to the throne of England, his power was formidable. But he frittered it away in quarrels with his sons, and with the clergy. Perhaps the most notable event of this reign was the murder of Henry's Archbishop, Thomas à Becket, whose murderers believed they were acting under orders of the king.

From the days of the Roman Empire, the clergy claimed the right to be tried by church courts for their crimes and not by the courts of law as other people. This privilege is referred to in our old law books as "Benefit of Clergy."

19

The practice had come to be so shamefully abused as to insure practical immunity from punishment by a priest that had committed a crime, no matter how glaring. This abuse Henry II. attempted to correct, and for this purpose he appointed his personal friend, Thomas à Becket, as Archbishop of Canterbury, and passed what is known in history as the Constitutions of Clarendon, which proposed to render priests amenable to the laws of the land for their misdeeds.

But Becket turned against the king, and displayed more stubbornness than any other primate had ever shown before, and so exasperated the king that he denounced the Archbishop in language that induced four knights to go immediately and murder the object of the king's wrath.

Mr. Dickens relates a very romantic story of the courtship, love, and marriage of the parents of Thomas à Becket; but it is too long for this brief sketch, and I must refer my readers to Dickens' Child's History of England.

It was this king that instituted trial by jury, and abolished the barbaric practice of trial by personal combat, which was nothing but forcing the parties to a law suit to *fight* each other, and it was supposed that the one that was in the right would beat his opponent.

Henry II. reigned thirty-five years, and died in the year 1189, when he was at war with all four of his sons, and was succeeded by his eldest son, as,

RICHARD I.

This king is better known as Richard Cœur de Leon, or Richard the Lion-Hearted, from his intrepid fighting with the Turks in the wars of the crusades. But there was an interval of a few months between Henry's death and Richard's coronation, during which time the queen mother, Eleanor, exercised acts of administration. One notable act of hers was the release of all the prisoners, "for the good of Henry's soul, inasmuch as she had learnt, in her own personal experience, that confinement is distasteful to mankind."

Richard I. was the very personification of mediæval chivalry, and was greatly beloved by his people. The historical novelists have shed a halo of glory about him that the unbiased historians have been obliged to disturb, and such a man now would be classed as a foolish knight-errant. Under his administration the Jews were more cruelly treated than they are now under the Russian government. The historian, Charles Knight, says: "Under Henry II. the Jews had only been robbed; under Richard I. they were ruthlessly massacred."

This Richard is known as the hero of the second and third crusades, and it was he, together with the king of France, that organized and managed the third crusade, and most of Richard's short reign was taken up in these eastern wars, while the administration of affairs in England was left with his brother John, called Lackland. It appears that the unpopularity of John at this time was due largely to the fact that he allowed no one to rob the Jews but himself. Sir Walter Scott's "Ivanhoe" is a fine portrayal of the times. Wamba, the jester, is made to refer to Richard as "*Dickon of the Broom,*" and Isaac of York was the type of Jewish money-lender that clung to John for protection from the populace, while he suffered *John* to rob him in return for this protection.

21

Richard I. died in the year 1199, of an arrow shot received while besieging a castle, and it is claimed by one historian that nothing in his life shows so clearly the strange inconsistency of his nature as the manner of his death. After being the hero of the Second and Third Crusades, Richard was shot by a boy in an unworthy fight over a paltry treasure found in the field of this castle; and the castle being taken after Richard received his wound, he ordered every inhabitant in the stronghold, except one, to be hanged. The boy that shot him was to be spared and pardoned by direct order of Richard. It was this mixture of ferocity and magnanimity that made up the sum total of Richard Cœur de Leon.

But the order was not respected, and after Richard was dead, the boy that aimed the arrow, whose name was Bertrand de Gurdun, was tortured to death in a manner too cruel to be related.

Richard I. was succeeded by his brother,

JOHN.

Although John had proved a traitor to his royal brother, he was designated by Richard as his successor, which is another instance of that strange magnanimity referred to above, and in this case nothing could have been more unwise, for of all the kings of England, from Alfred the Great down to the present time, there is not one other so universally execrated and despised as this same John.

The historian Miles says that Genghis Khan, after shedding more human blood than any other individual since the dawn of history, ordered forty young maidens to be slain at the door of his tent the moment of his death, to minister unto him in the spirit world: The same historian says that Catherine de Medici instigated the massacre of St. Bartholomew to hide her guilt in the attempted assassination of a single man. We know from Holy Writ that Herod caused the ruthless murder of all the male infants of Bethlehem, to remove a possible but unknown rival: And Josephus says that this same monster, when he was about to die, attempted, by diabolical finesse, to gather all the most honored men in Judea into one vast building, that he might have them all slain, believing that his memory would be glorified by unprecedented renown as a destroyer of human life, and, as he said, that his soul might depart this life in good company. And it is said that he was balked in this horrible design only because his soldiery refused to perform the execution. But posterity has gone farther toward forgiving Genghis Khan, and Catherine de Medici, and Herod of Jewry, for these awful deeds of wickedness, than it has King John for his pure villainy.

A religious writer of the times said: "Christ and His saints slept during the reign of John." A bolder writer of that period said: "Vile as hell itself is, it is yet defiled by the still viler presence of John." And Green, the historian, thinks posterity fully upholds this writer in his terrible arraignment.

Yet it was under John, in the year 1215, that Magna Carta, the Great Charter, was first granted to the English people, the very foundation of English liberty. But John is due no credit for this concession. It was wrested from him after years of desperate strife; and it was no sooner signed than he wished to abolish it, and actually obtained the sanction of the Pope to disclaim the act, as extorted under duress. So the war between him and his nobles was continued, and John died in the year 1216, still resisting Magna Carta.

Hardy, the English antiquarian, has unearthed from the ancient archives of London, an order of King John, written at this time, which shows something of the spiteful nature of this royal monster. The order runs thus:

"The king to all his bailiffs and faithful people who may view these letters. Know ye, that the citizens of London in common have seditiously and deceitfully withdrawn themselves from our service and fealty; and therefore we command you that when any of their servants or chattels pass through your districts, ye do offer them all the reproaches in your power, even as ye would to our enemies; and in testimony hereof we send you these our letters patent."

Upon the death of John, it was proposed to seat a Frenchman upon the English throne, and the barons actually invited Louis, a son of the French king Philip Augustus, to come over to England and assume the royal sceptre; but blood is thicker than water. In this instance it proved stronger than the terrible memory of the wickedness of King John. The nation bristled with patriotism too ardent to be resisted by the barons, and John's young son, a mere child, was crowned king, as

HENRY III.

This king's reign was the longest in English history, except Victoria's and George III.'s, and covered a period of fifty-six years.

24

But for the nightmare-memory of his father's reign, the tyranny of Henry III. would have been intolerable; for this long, dreary reign was one continued struggle of the people for the recognition and enlargement of Magna Carta, and, as a result of this struggle, the common people began to have a voice in the councils of the nation, and the House of Commons came into existence. The people learned that the proper and successful way to redress grievances was not to *fight* the king, but to withhold supplies from him, and this they did by a simple appearing law, which reads as follows:

"No scutage or aid shall be imposed in our kingdom, unless by the common council of our kingdom."

This little law has proved the most effective curb to kingly tyranny that has ever been contrived by the lawmakers in all time; and it simply means that the people alone ought to have the power to levy taxes.

It was in the year 1220, while Henry III. was still a minor, that he commenced the rebuilding of Westminster Abbey, which had been the coronation church of the kings of England since the days of Harold, Last of the Saxon Kings, but which had fallen into decay and ruin. The Abbey was practically completed in the next reign; though it has been altered and beautified by many succeeding kings, especially by Henry VII. This famous structure is now more famous and celebrated than the Kremlin of the Russians, or the Mosque of St. Sophia, or the Alhambra of the Moors, and is the resting place for the ashes of the kings as far back as Edward the Confessor. It was from this scene of magnificence in death that Washington Irving turned in sadness and said, "When I look upon the tombs of the great, every emotion of envy dies within me."

Henry III. died in the year 1272, and was succeeded by his son,

EDWARD I.

You will recall that we have already spoken of three kings named Edward,—that is, Edward the Elder, Edward the Martyr, and Edward the Confessor; but Edward, son of Henry III., whose reign began in 1272, is known in English history as Edward I. They did not begin to designate the kings by Roman numerals till after the Norman Conquest, though nobody has ever explained (to me) just why. However, this is the first of the three Edwards we now have in direct succession.

It was under this king that England attempted to subjugate Scotland, and Sir William Wallace came into the limelight as a warrior. Edward had this celebrated hero hanged, drawn and quartered, which act of barbarity has had the effect to immortalize Wallace as a patriot, and, in some parts of the world, at least, to brand Edward with infamy. The author of "The Scottish Chiefs" accuses Edward's young queen of falling desperately in love with Wallace; but the story seems to have no foundation in fact. This is a solitary instance where a woman will sometimes commit a meaner act than a man will. The vilest man I have ever seen would shrink from attributing infidelity to a young and virtuous lady, even though not the queen, as he would shrink from blasphemy; but here we have the authoress of a great and immensely popular book doing this very act, altogether without proof, or even suspicion, just to add emphasis to her partisan argument. I say this though my sympathies are with the Scots in that heroic struggle, and I am always ready to admit that women, as a rule, are infinitely better than men.

Edward I., before his accession to the throne, went to the Holy Land on a crusade. He captured the City of Nazareth, and, in his zeal, so unlike our ideas of Christian charity, killed every Turk found in the town. This king was a man of violent temper, and was brutally cruel to all who opposed him, yet history accords him the reputation of being the first English king to rank as a statesman of high order; and some historians regard him as the founder of constitutional liberty in England; and it is certain that he is the first king to concede voluntarily the principles of Magna Carta.

In the year 1307, King Edward I. died, while on an invasion of Scotland, and it is said that he caused his son to kneel at his bedside and swear that his bones should be boiled clean in a caldron, and carried in front of the English army till Scotland should be subdued. But if that oath had been kept, the king's bones would still occupy their station of honor in the van of that august column whose banners never lose the sun's light; for Scotland has never been subdued.

Edward I. was succeeded by his son,

EDWARD II.

This king is referred to by more than one historian as "the despicable Edward II." It was he that the Bruce overwhelmed at Bannockburn, the decisive battle that secured the independence of Scotland. This king had been committed to prison in his youth by his father, for misdemeanors, and as a man he was no improvement on his boyhood. He was not a cruel king, but was weak and faithless, and never gained the hearts of his subjects.

Edward II. had a mania for dissolute favorites, and it seems that most of his troubles were directly due to this unwisdom. One of his foreign favorites, named Piers Gaveston, was in the habit of attaching contemptuous nicknames to the great and powerful lords, such epithets as, "The Black Dog," "The Old Hog," and "The Jew," which his master thought extremely funny and a high order of wit; but he drew down upon himself the hatred of a class so powerful that the king could not save his favorite, and he was judicially murdered by the outraged nobles.

Famine and pestilence followed the great victories of Bruce over the English, and added to the general discontent. Then as a climax to all the king's troubles, his queen, who was Isabella, daughter of Philip Le Bel, King of France, turned against her lord, went to France on a visit, and refused to return. She is credited by the historians with living a scandalous life in Paris with her English lover, Roger Mortimer; and when she did return to England, it was at the head of an army hostile to her husband.

With Isabella was the king's son, a lad thirteen years old, who was made the tool of his designing mother, and all England rallied about this boy, and drove the king and his unpopular favorites from power. The favorites were killed, and the king placed in prison in Kenilworth Castle; while the young kinglet was crowned, and Mortimer and the faithless queen were supreme in the State.

Mortimer conceived the idea that he would be safer in his illicit intercourse with the queen if Edward were dead; so he hired two human brutes to murder him in a manner so horrible that few historians have ventured to describe it; for there are limits imposed by decency that human nature itself refuses to pass, and beyond which even the truth must be suppressed.

More than five hundred years after the death of Edward II., the correspondence that occurred between the king and queen at the time when she was living in Paris with Mortimer, her lover, came to light when the letters were found in the French archives, and revealed the royal "carbuncle" in all its hideousness.

Edward II. was the first heir apparent to the throne to be called Prince of Wales, a title of honor that the eldest son of the kings enjoys to this day. The stubborn Welsh had claimed from time immemorial that they had the right to a king of true Welsh stock. The people of Wales were the remnant of the ancient Britons, and had never submitted to Saxon, Anglo-Saxon, nor Norman rule, and boasted through their poets that:

"Since from the east hither Angles and Saxons came to land,—since o'er the broad seas mighty war-smiths sought Britain, the Welsh overcame the most bold this earth obtained."

So it came about that Edward I., knowing of the universal objection to him as a ruler among the Welsh, by what he thought a shrewd trick, promised the Welsh people that he would give them a prince who was a native of Wales. And to fulfill this promise (in his own way), sent the queen into Wales a short time before a child was to be born to her. In due time the prince was born, and the king held the child up before a great concourse of people and proclaimed him Prince of Wales. The king had his "rooters" distributed among the people to shout for joy; but the Welsh looked on in sullen disapproval, refusing to be placated by so sorry a ruse, and only became reconciled when a real king of Welsh blood succeeded to the throne, as we shall see in the accession of the House of Tudor more than two hundred years after the birth of Edward II.

It remains to be stated that neither Queen Isabella, nor her guilty lover long enjoyed the prestige this revolution gained for them; for the young king soon learned that their scandalous conduct was bringing reproach on him and his court, and he had Mortimer arrested, tried for treason, condemned, and executed; while with more of justice than filial duty, he caused his mother to be placed under mild prison restraint for the remainder of her life.

It was in the year 1327 that Edward II. died, and even before his death, but in the same year, he was succeeded by his son, a boy of thirteen years, as

EDWARD III.

This Edward was infinitely better than his father, and more successful than his grandfather, and his want of great ability was largely compensated for by his honesty and evident desire to please his people. After his death there was an attempt to have his name handed down in the history of England as Edward the Great; but the effort was abortive, and of all the long line of English kings Alfred alone is thus honored.

Edward III. was the founder of the Order of the Garter, the most celebrated order of mediæval chivalry, and the historian Green gives the following incident in connection with its origin: Edward III. gave a great tournament at Windsor, at which there were present many of the greatest lords and ladies of the land. During the exercises the Duchess of Salisbury lost her garter, which fell to the ground, much to the merriment of the spectators, and the lady's own chagrin and discomfiture. The king, seeing the embarrassment of the Duchess, gallantly stepped forward, took up the garter, and, handing it to its owner, said: *"Honi soit qui mal y pense,"* that is, *Evil be to him that evil thinketh.* This sentence was adopted as the motto of the Order of the Garter.

The reign of Edward III. was filled with wars with Scotland and with France, and it was he that fought and won the celebrated battle of Crecy; but his wars with Scotland were not so successful. During this reign that terrible scourge, the Black Death, destroyed about one-third of the population of Europe. The historian Miles says that this was the greatest calamity that ever befell the human race.

Edward III. reigned a full half century, his being the fourth longest reign in the catalogue of English kings. His eldest son, Edward, so well known as the Black

Prince, so named from his black armor he wore, was the idol of the English people, and they fondly looked to him as their future king; but this prince died in 1376, and was buried in Canterbury, and his mailed effigy is to be seen there at this day.

We are to remember Edward III. as the common ancestor of the rival Houses of York and Lancaster of whom we are to hear so much presently. It is not often that a line of facts can be more clearly and more briefly stated in verse than in prose; but Shakespeare has done this in the following lines:

> "Edward the third, my lords, had seven sons,
> First, Edward the Black Prince, Prince of Wales;
> The second, William of Hatfield, and the third,
> Lionel Duke of Clarence; next to whom
> Was John of Gaunt, the Duke of Lancaster;
> The fifth was Edmund Langley, Duke of York;
> The sixth was Thomas of Woodstock, Duke of Gloucester,
> William of Windsor was the seventh and last."

Strange to say, the historian Lancaster ignores William of Hatfield, and refers to Lionel, Duke of Clarence, as the second son.

Since the Black Prince had died before his father, it was feared by the people that on the death of Edward III., John of Gaunt, the most vigorous of all the sons of his father, but very unpopular (because he was foreign born,—he having been born in the city of Ghent, pronounced Gaunt by the common people), would seize the crown, and exclude the young son of the Black Prince. So when Edward III. died in the year 1377, and John of

Gaunt made no effort to supplant his brother's heir, but, on the contrary, assisted his nephew with all his splendid ability, there was great rejoicing, and the nickname, *Gaunt*, instead of a reproach, was worn by this great statesman to the end of his long and useful life as a title of honor, as:

"Old John of Gaunt, time-honored Lancaster."

Edward III. was succeeded by his grandson, the infant son of the Black Prince, as

RICHARD II.

This king was but eleven years of age when he came to the throne, but, as the son of the popular idol, he was received in a burst of approbation. But as the old unpopularity of John of Gaunt began to disappear, the young king began to show his jealousy, and his own popularity waned, and it was but a few short years before he had completely alienated his people from him.

Most historians describe Richard II. as a cruel, cowardly, and unjust prince; though there are some that give him a better name. It is true that he protected Wycklif, and encouraged Chaucer; but, as a whole, he was a miserable failure. Lord Lytton has said that there was not a coward in the line of the Plantagenet dynasty; but most historians regard this Richard II. something very like a coward, when you scratch through the outer covering of "bluff."

It is true, nevertheless, that under this king the House of Commons forged further towards the front than it had

33

ever before attained. This is true, however, because Richard II. was not a strong king to prevent it. It is the history of constitutional freedom in England that this principle always lost ground under strong kings, and gained under the weak, which is but another way of stating the truth that:

"Eternal vigilance is the price of liberty."

Richard II. was deposed, and the historian Charles Knight facetiously says that this is the one great reform accomplished in this reign.

It was during this reign that the seeds of the Wars of the Roses were sown, for, during Richard's minority, he was pulled and dragged around by his uncles, and the jealousies of these uncles were transmitted to their children, and they gained in momentum till they culminated in civil war.

Richard had his uncle Gloucester beheaded; he banished Henry Bolingbroke, the beloved son of John of Gaunt. He did not dare to touch old John himself, now the most popular man in England, but the moment John of Gaunt was dead, Richard seized on all his fortune and confiscated it to his own use.

Bolingbroke, hearing of his father's death, and of the king's act of robbery, boldly came back to England, and demanded his right to the title of Duke of Lancaster, and his father's fortune. Richard was in Ireland when Henry landed, and the people were thus emboldened to flock to Henry's standard; for the robbery of old John of Gaunt was more than they would stand for.

Richard came home from Ireland, to find himself deserted by commons, nobles, and Welsh. At first he showed such a bold front that men who had despised him half forgave him for the past. It is at this time that Shakespeare puts these high-sounding words in Richard's mouth:

> "Not all the water in the, rough, rude sea
> Can wash the balm off from an annointed king."

Richard shut himself up in a castle with some half a dozen noblemen, and impotently railed at Henry, who was surrounded by an army of twenty thousand men. He expressed great surprise and indignation that Henry's messenger did not fall down on his knees to him, and he sent Henry a mandatory order to quit the realm and disperse his bands, or unconditionally surrender.

Shakespeare quotes this message thus:

> "Tell Bolingbroke—for yond methinks he stands—
> That every stride he makes upon my land
> Is dangerous treason: he is come to open
> The purple testament of bleeding war;
> But ere the crown he looks for live in peace,
> Ten thousand bloody crowns of mothers' sons
> Shall ill become the flower of England's face,
> Change the complexion of her maid-pale peace
> To scarlet indignation, and bedew
> Her pastures' grass with faithful English blood."

But it required but very little water to wash the balm off of Richard; and "the purple testament of bleeding war" remained closed. Within a few days after these brave words, he humbly crouched at the feet of Henry, Duke of Lancaster, resigned his crown, and declared that if he had the naming of his successor, he would, of all men, name Henry of Lancaster, called Bolingbroke.

Shakespeare expresses the same thought in statelier phrase; he depicts the Duke of York coming to Henry as a messenger from Richard, and thus delivering himself:

"Great Duke of Lancaster, I come to thee
From plume-plucked Richard, who with willing soul
Adopts thee heir, and his high sceptre yields
To the possession of thy Royal hand."

Shakespeare's "Richard II." and "Henry IV." are wonderfully true to history, as are his "Henry VI." and "Richard III.," and these latter two tragedies taken together make the best history of the Wars of the Roses that we have. It is true, the events of decades are crowded into single acts, and highly colored for stage effect; but we get it all, as in no other work.

When Richard II. was deposed, he was committed to prison at Pomfret, and his young queen was sent back to France whence she came, and she never saw her husband again. Richard's final fate is unknown. He was succeeded in 1399 by

HENRY IV.

With the accession of Henry IV. the quarrel between the Houses of York and Lancaster became more bitter. The House of York had adopted the white rose as its badge, and the distinguishing insignia of the House of Lancaster was the red rose. The embers smouldered for half a century, and in 1450 burst into a raging flame, which for thirty-five years thereafter continued with terrible vigor, and practically annihilated the nobility of England; and from the badges of the contending factions, these wars are known in history as The Wars of the Roses.

Henry IV. was an usurper of the kingly office; but his usurpation was with the aid and consent of a vast majority of the English people. This king did many wicked and cruel acts, but one thing he did has shed lustre on his name for all time. He was the first English monarch to place under the ban pillage by his soldiery, and no king since his time has permitted it, except at the expense of his reputation.

Here the temptation to wander off into Shakespeare's "Henry IV." is almost overwhelming. It is there we first meet Sir John Falstaff, Dame Quickly, The Boar's Head Tavern in Eastcheap, Hotspur, and a host of other celebrities of the fancy that are better known than real historic personages. An old writer, speaking of Henry IV., has said: "History, strictly so called,—the history derived from the Rolls and Statutes,—'must pale its ineffectual fire' in the sunlight of the poet."

But the blot on the fair name of Henry IV. is that he was the first persecutor of the Reformers, or rather the forerunners of the Reformers; for at this time the followers of Wycklif were called Lollards.

This king reigned fourteen years, and was succeeded upon his death, in the year 1413, by his wild and wayward son, the companion of Falstaff, the frequenter of Eastcheap, as

HENRY V.

At the very outset of his reign, Henry V. dismissed his old associates with small pensions, and ordered them to never come into his presence again; and he became at once a wise and strong king, whipped the French almost from the face of the earth, and raised England to first place among the nations of Europe. But Henry V.'s best history is the history of the great battle of Agincourt, where his army destroyed a French force ten times their number, and where the flower of the nobility of France perished.

Yet this fearful sacrifice of human life was all for naught but to satisfy false ambition, and had no object but to assert an indomitable will; nor were there any permanent results of this destructive war, except the perpetuation of hatred between England and France.

Knight's Popular History, quoting from the old historian Mackintosh, says: "Whatever admiration we may feel for the bravery, fortitude, and self-reliance of Henry V., we must rank him among the guilty possessors of kingly power; and make a large abatement from the vaunted generosity of one who 'lay in wait for the best opportunity of aggrandizing himself at the expense of his distracted neighbors; as if nations were only more numerous gangs of banditti, instead of being communities formed only for the observance and enforcement of justice.' "

Like Tamerlane, Henry V. lives in history as the incarnation of the malignant spirit of conquest.

Sir Richard Whittington, London's most renowned Lord Mayor, flourished during this reign, and the story of his life, as boy and man, has been an inspiration to countless thousands of youth. What child has not heard:

> "Turn again Whittington,
> Thrice Lord Mayor of London."

Most historians cast doubt on the story of Dick Whittington and his famous cat; but it is significant that in the year 1862, workmen, while remodeling an old house at Gloucester that belonged to the Whittington family, found a stone of fifteenth century workmanship, on which appeared in bas-relief the figure of a boy nursing a cat in his arms.

Henry V. died in 1422, and it seems that historians and political economists are agreed that his death was a greater stroke of fortune for England than the great victories recorded in his reign; for he was fast developing a kind of strength that boded ill for English liberty.

During this short reign the Lollards, the followers of Wycklif, were persecuted with extreme severity, and many suffered martyrdom. The last will and testament of this king is still preserved among the royal archives of England. Its last clause is a pitiful prayer, thus:

"Jesu mercy and gramercy Ladie Marie help. R. H."

This king was succeeded by his infant son, as

HENRY VI.

And now it was that the spirit of liberty had an opportunity to get on its "feet" again; for Henry VI. was not only a mere baby when his father died, but he developed into a weak and insignificant man. His reign covered a period of thirty-nine years, and after his minority was passed he was under "petticoat" government. His queen, a daughter of the titular king of Naples, brought him no dower, and for her he was obliged to give up much of England's valuable possessions on the continent. This strong-minded and unscrupulous queen was the real ruler of England, till her authority was wrested from her by the nobles.

During this reign England lost most of her possessions in France; the brilliant conquests of Henry V. passing as most ill-gotten gains pass. It was in this reign that Joan of Arc suffered. O the pity of it! The historian Green tells us that as her spirit left her body, a common English soldier turned to a comrade and said: *"We are lost: we have burnt a Saint."*

This act of barbarity has probably brought more blushes of shame to English cheeks than any other one act ever perpetrated by English authority.

In Francis Palgrave's "Visions of England," there is a beautiful little poem called Jeanne D'arc. It is not out of place to repeat the last stanza here:

> "Poor sweet maid of Domremy,
>   In thine innocence secure,
> Heed not what men say of thee,
>   The buffoon and his jest impure!
> Nor care if thy name, young martyr,
>   Be the star of thy country's story:
> 'Mid the white-robed host of the heavens
>   Thou hast more than glory!"

It was during this reign, in the year 1450, that the Wars of the Roses, that terrible struggle between the Houses of York and Lancaster, broke out into open violence, and the Earl of Warwick, known as the king-maker, came into prominence. He took the side of the Yorkists against Henry VI., and after he had deposed Henry, and York offended him, he again set Henry on the throne. It is he that Queen Margaret refers to as:

"Proud setter up and puller down of kings!"

Henry VI. was really an incompetent, and he was deposed in the year 1462, and with him passed the House of Lancaster. He was succeeded by the representative of the House of York, in the person of

EDWARD IV.

We are now in the very heyday of the Wars of the Roses. Henry VI. was the last king of the House of Lancaster, and Edward IV. was the first of the House of York.

We are to remember that the House of Lancaster sprang from John of Gaunt, who was the *fourth* son of Edward III., while the House of York had its origin in Edmund Langley, Duke of York, and *fifth* son of the same Edward. This statement, on its face, would appear to give the House of Lancaster the better right, and this is true if we consider the male line only; but the House of York had another card up its sleeve. The Salic Law had been repealed. The third son of Edward III., Lionel, Duke of Clarence, had an only daughter, and she intermarried with her cousin of York, and it was through this female line that the House of York claimed precedence over the descendants of John of Gaunt, the fourth son. This reasoning convinced the Earl of Warwick, the king-maker, and won him over to the side of Edward IV., though he, himself, was more nearly related in blood to the House of Lancaster.

One of the first acts of Edward IV. was to send Warwick as an ambassador to the King of France, to negotiate a marriage with the French king's sister. But while this negotiation was going on, Edward married Elizabeth Woodville, the widow of Lord Grey, an English lady; and it was she who introduced the name *Elizabeth* into the royal family of England, and we shall see later on that her daughter, also named Elizabeth, married King Henry VII., who was the grandfather of Elizabeth the Great Queen,—but I am anticipating.

We are told that when Warwick heard that Edward IV. had mocked him by marrying another woman, he swore vengeance against Edward, and came back to England as a friend to the deposed Henry VI. It was at this time that Warwick is quoted as saying:

> "I was the chief that raised him to the crown,
> And I'll be chief to bring him down again:
> Not that I pity Henry's misery,
> But seek revenge on Edward's mockery."

No king of the House of York ever reigned quietly in England. This Edward's reign was troubled and bloody, and no advance either in learning, or in the arts, is noticeable under him.

It is matter of wonder to most people how it was possible, even in those days, for great families, like the Houses of York and Lancaster, to destroy each other, and not be called to account. This is explained by the fact that the party in power had a ready instrument of torture always at hand, that waited the king's beck and will to bring its cruel engines into play, to crush truth and innocence with shameless affrontery. *This instrument of torture was the Church!* Some ten years ago, a high North Carolina official made the unguarded statement that, "The Church has always been on the side of human slavery." Our good people from mountain to sea, rose in their righteous indignation, and branded this official as a blasphemer. But if you would scan the list of those who were loudest in their condemnation, it is to be feared that but few students of history would be found among them.

But the Reformation has changed all that, and such a charge against the Church of the present day would be unfair.

Of all the preaching since that of the Apostle Peter, down to the present day, there has been no more convincing argument for the divinity of Jesus Christ than that His doctrines have survived the personnel of the Church in the Middle Ages.

The Church was a favorite instrument of Edward IV. when he wished to put a great enemy out of the way; though this charge applies to Edward's predecessors probably with more justice than to him; for just at this time the nobility had so nearly all perished that the commons began to wield an influence not so easily controlled.

It is wearisome to dwell upon the dreary, bloody annals of the York kings; hence we will hasten on to the description of Richard III., Edward's brother, the most wicked monster that has ever worn the crown of England, —for we must dispose of him no matter how disagreeable.

Edward IV. died in 1483, and was succeeded by his infant son, as

EDWARD V.

This child was titular king for the space of eleven weeks. He and his younger brother, Richard, were shut up in the tower by order of their uncle Richard, brother of the late king, and there ruthlessly murdered. Richard is said to have procured this foul murder, by the agency of one James Tyrrell, and Shakespeare credits Tyrrell with reporting the horrible crime thus:

> "The tyrannous and bloody deed is done,
> The most arch act of piteous massacre
> That ever yet this land was guilty of.
> Dighton and Forest, whom I did suborn
> To do this ruthless piece of butchery,
> Although they are flesh'd villains, bloody dogs,
> Melting with tenderness and kind compassion
> Wept like two children in their death's sad stories.
> 'Lo, thus,' quoth Dighton, 'lay those tender babes':
> 'Thus, thus,' quoth Forest, 'girding one another
> Within their innocent alabaster arms:
> Their lips were four red roses on a stalk,
> Which in their summer beauty kiss'd each other.' "

As soon as the boys were dead, Richard seized the crown, and was acknowledged

RICHARD III.

This third and last of the York kings was a strong character, but he was a cruel and wicked monster. He seems to have *gloried* in his wickedness. He caused the murder of his brother Clarence, his own wife, and some half dozen others that were in his way to the throne, and last of all the two sons of his dead brother, and is quoted as boasting about it thus:

> "But then I sigh; and with a piece of scripture,
> Tell them that God bids us do good for evil:
> And thus I clothe my naked villainy
> With old odds and ends stolen out of holy writ
> And seem a saint, when most I play the devil."

As soon as it was known that Richard had caused the murder of his two nephews, the whole nation rose in rebellion against Richard in a storm of horrified indignation. The rebellion was headed by Henry Tudor, Earl of Richmond, who defeated the forces of Richard, and Richard himself was slain on Bosworth Field in 1485.

In Shakespeare's tragedy, "Richard III.," we are given a highly tragic account of this battle, and especially of the camps of the opposing armies the night before the battle. We are shown Richard and Henry sleeping in their separate tents, while the ghosts of those Richard had murdered appear, and to the sleeping Richard they say:

> "Let me sit heavy on thy soul to-morrow!"

But the historians tell us that, on Bosworth Field, Richard exhibited bravery worthy of a better cause. He entered the battle feeling that his army was invincible; but all at once he was deserted and left to his fate. This is the time and place that Shakespeare represents Richard, after being unhorsed, as shouting:

> "A horse, a horse, my kingdom for a horse!"

But what he actually said and did, was to cry: "Treason, treason," and to rush madly up to the Earl of Richmond, when he fell while trying to cut Richmond from his horse.

As the crown, bruised and soiled, rolled from Richard's head, it was taken up then and there, and placed on the head of Henry Tudor, Earl of Richmond, with a great shout of: "*Long Live King Henry!*" This was

HENRY VII.

With King Richard III., passed the House of York, the Plantagenet dynasty, and the feudal system of England.

It is only fair to say that if I now fail to give my young readers something of interest, it will be my own fault; for the history of the House of Tudor is the pith and kernel of English history. Both writers and readers are apt to dwell long and fondly on this period; for it is a relief to pass from the acrid recitals of the Plantagenets to the fertile story of the Tudors, rich and ripe in human interest. And though the Tudor line is deeply stained with blood, its spice and snap are preferred to the maudlin story of the House of Stuart, and the insipid annals of the House of Hanover.

Henry VII. was the son of a Welsh nobleman, but his mother was a granddaughter of John of Gaunt, and he was the last living representative of the House of Lancaster. At the suggestion of Henry's first Parliament, he married Elizabeth of York, a daughter of Edward IV., and she was the only living eligible of the House of York.

A Thousand Years With Royalty.

The Wars of the Roses were at an end: The Red Rose and the White Rose were entwined in one wreath; while the Welsh were reconciled, and have remained loyal to the government from the accession of Henry VII. to the present day; and Wales has contributed its quota of great men to the British nation, including the present Chancellor, David Lloyd-George.

Champlin, the historian and cyclopedist, described Henry VII. thus: "He was a wise and prudent king, with a great knack at money-making, which was not always by fair means." It was this king that so materially beautified Westminster Abbey. The *Chapel of Henry VII.*, so justly famous as an ornament to the great Abbey, was the work of this Henry.

In the year 1502, Henry VII.'s daughter Margaret married James IV., King of Scotland, a fact to be remembered as the link connecting the House of Stuart to the royal line of England, and by which the Stuarts inherited the crown of England, after the failure of the Tudor line, which ended with Queen Elizabeth, just a hundred years after this Scottish marriage of Margaret.

The most beautiful lyric in Palgrave's "Visions of England" is based on the subject of Margaret's marriage. I quote two stanzas of it:

> "Love who art above us all,
>   Guard the treasure on her way,
> Flower of England, fair and tall,
>   Maiden-wise, and maiden gay,
> As her northward path she goes;
> Daughter of the double rose.

47

> Look with twofold grace on her,
>   Who from twofold root has grown,
> Flower of York and Lancaster
>   Now to grace another throne,
> Rose in Scotland's garden set,—
> Britain's only Margaret."

It may be of interest to note here, that this Margaret's son has been immortalized by Sir Walter Scott as the James FitzJames of "Lady of the Lake,"—he that fought the sword duel with Roderick Dhu, at Coilantogle's Ford, where we are told:

> "Ill fared it then with Rhoderick Dhu,
> That on the ground his targe he threw,
> Whose brazen studs and tough bull hide,
> Had death so often dashed aside;
> For trained abroad his arms to wield,
> Fitz-James' blade was sword and shield."

Margaret's second marriage was with Lord Angus the Douglas, and thus she was the grandmother of both Mary, Queen of Scots, and her husband, Lord Darnley, the parents of James I., who succeeded Queen Elizabeth. I have digressed into this ramification of the royal line to show the kinship of the Norman line to the House of Stuart.

It was during the reign of Henry VII. that the great Columbus discovered America, under the auspices of Ferdinand and Isabella, king and queen of Spain; and Henry sent out the Cabots, John and Sebastian, father and son, the first discoverers of our continent of North America.

Henry's reign was beset with impostors, claiming to be Dukes of York, representatives of the last reigning family, and many poor, simple people lost their lives by joining the fortunes of these impostors, against the king.

It was Henry's custom, in punishing these rebellions, to hang the guilty parties on gallowses supposed to be suited to the culprit's station in life: that is to say, a rebel who occupied a high station in society would be hanged on a high gallows; while a common laborer would be hanged on a low scaffold. Speaking of this, Mr. Dickens quaintly says: "Hang high, hang low, hanging is very much the same to the person hanged."

Henry VII.'s eldest son, Arthur, Prince of Wales, was married at the age of fifteen, to Catherine of Aragon, a daughter of Ferdinand and Isabella of Spain, but Arthur died within a few months. Instead of returning to her parents, the young widow was retained in England as a widow, for six years, waiting for the second son of English royalty to arrive at the ripe and marriageable age of fifteen; at which time the king procured a dispensation from the Pope for Arthur's widow to marry young Henry, the brother of her first youthful bridegroom. This wedding was arranged, but not consummated till after the death of Henry VII. We shall see in the next reign what untold trouble was brought about by these child-marriages.

In the year 1509, Henry VII. died, and was quietly succeeded by his son, who was the first sovereign to assume the royal office without any dispute of his title since the accession of Edward III., nearly two hundred years before. This new king was

HENRY VIII.

This is the king who, in playful mood, knighted that part of the beef that we still call *Sirloin*.

This reign is usually considered one of the most important in all English history. But great as are the reforms that have grown out of the reign of Henry VIII., not one is due to any virtue in the king himself. Most of these reforms came of changes Henry inaugurated for his own selfish purposes. He destroyed the power of the Pope in England only to make himself Pope. He broke up the great monasteries, that his coffers might be enriched with their spoils. He championed the Protestant cause, for the reason that the Catholic Church had laid him under an interdict.

But for Henry's quarrel with the Pope, he would have most probably stamped out the Protestant cause, though, in doing so, he would have sacrificed tens of thousands of his subjects at the stake.

Most of Henry VIII.'s time was taken up in marrying wives, and either divorcing them or cutting off their heads. His first wife, as we have seen, was Catherine of Aragon, his brother Arthur's widow. He married her at the age of eighteen, while she was his senior by a number of years. After Henry had lived with Catherine fifteen years, he pretended that his conscience had "crept too close" to him, at the thought of having married the widow of his dead brother. (The idea of Henry VIII. having a conscience!) Shakespeare puts it in the mouth of the Earl of Surrey as saying, "The king's conscience has crept too close to another lady." This was doubtless true, for just at the time Henry began to feel these qualms of conscience, he also began to heap honors upon one of the queen's maids-in-waiting, the beautiful and vivacious daughter of Sir Thomas Boleyn, famous in history as Anne Boleyn.

The Pope refused his assent to Henry's proposal for a divorce from Catherine, and Henry defied the Pope, and put servile judges on the bench to do his liking.

Still the divorce suit dragged on; for great as was Henry's power, not yet was all England willing to embrace this shameful injustice to Queen Catherine, to satisfy the king's evanescent fancy. He dismissed his ministers, railed on the judges, and all the time paid assiduous court to Anne Boleyn. It was at this time, that Anne, who pretended great love for the queen and sorrow for her distress, is quoted by the poet as moralizing thus:

> ".   .   .   Verily,
> I swear, 'tis better to be lowly born,
> And range with humble livers in content,
> Than to be perk'd up in a glistening grief,
> And wear a golden sorrow."

And Anne is represented as delivering such fine speeches as this in commiseration of Queen Catherine's misfortune, while she, herself, was plotting to complete the queen's downfall.

Henry's impatience at the slow process of the divorce court broke all bounds, and he secretly married Anne Boleyn six months before the decree of divorce was issued.

At last the divorce was forthcoming, and Anne was crowned queen; and some three months later a daughter was born to her, whom they named Elizabeth.

Love that is not founded in respect and trust is usually short-lived. Henry's love for Anne Boleyn was not of this type, but partook more of the nature of animal lust; and, as was quite natural, was soon followed by satiety and neglect.

A Thousand Years With Royalty.

After Henry had tired of his butterfly wife, we are told that weeks would pass without his once calling her to speak to him. Her sprightly temper and natural vivacity resented the king's cruel neglect, and she began to get "gay" with the young nobles about the court. All at once, and without a warning frown, Henry ordered Anne to her trial for infidelity.

In the British museum there is to be seen a touching letter in Anne Boleyn's own handwriting, written to Henry by her while she was in the Tower awaiting her trial. In this letter, she stoutly maintains her innocence, and tells the king in splendid language, and with a spirit worthy of her illustrious daughter, that he never would have suspected her of a crime that had never entered her mind, but that he had become enamored of another woman. I would like much to copy this great letter in full, but it is too long for the promised scope of my story.

Anne was convicted, though without sufficient evidence, and her beautiful neck was severed on the block.

Henry mourned the respectable period of two weeks after Anne's death, and married Jane Seymour. This wife gave Henry a son, while Catherine and Anne Boleyn had only given him a daughter each; so Jane Seymour had the good fortune to die a natural death. But most people think she would not have been so fortunate had she deferred the matter a little longer.

Thomas Cromwell was at this time Henry's Prime Minister, and he persuaded the king that this time he should make a policy marriage, and to aid him in his argument, Cromwell hired a clever artist to "doctor" up a picture of Anne of Cleves, a great, fat German lady, and the artist did his doctoring so well that the king went into ecstasies over the beauty of the picture, and decided that he wanted the lady Anne for his fourth queen, and wanted her at once. So Henry sent an embassy with his proposal of marriage to Anne of Cleves, and instructed his agents that they were to bring the lady directly to London; and this was done without unnecessary delay.

But when Henry saw the original of the delusive picture he went into another sort of ecstasy, and this time he swore vengeance on the head of Cromwell. It was only the threat of war with Germany that induced Henry to keep his contract and carry out the wedding agreement.

So Henry VIII. married Anne of Cleves, and divorced Anne of Cleves, and ruined Thomas Cromwell, all in the year. This decree of divorce was easily obtained, for by this time the courts had become shamelessly servile to the will of the king. The decree naïvely recited that, "Either party was free to marry again"; and this Henry proceeded to do at once.

Queen number five was Catherine Howard. Henry lived with her fifteen months, and on several occasions publicly gave thanks for his domestic felicity. But then it came out that this Catherine, before her marriage with the king, had lived a scandalously unchaste life; so she was promptly sent to *her* death.

By this time the great ladies began to be wary of this royal bait, and when Henry made an offer to an Italian princess, that lady thanked him for the compliment, but said she preferred to keep her head. After some casting about, Henry married a widow named Catherine Parr, and she outlived her lord.

A Thousand Years With Royalty.

Henry VIII. was the father of three children: Mary, daughter of Catherine of Aragon; Elizabeth, daughter of Anne Boleyn; and Edward, son of Jane Seymour. They all three held the sceptre of England, as shall directly hereafter appear.

The rise, flourish, and fall of Henry's two celebrated prime ministers, the great Cardinal Woolsey, and later Thomas Cromwell, give us a study in human ambition, and emphasize the Biblical injunction: *"Put not your trust in Princes."* It is curious to know that Woolsey fell because of his opposition to Henry's marriage with Anne Boleyn; while Cromwell's fall was due to his advocacy of the marriage with Anne of Cleves. Woolsey recognizes the cause of his fall, when in his last interview with his friend and pupil, and his destined successor, he is represented as saying in reference to Anne Boleyn:

"There was the weight that pulled me down."

It was just after Woolsey's arrest that Shakespeare gives that famous soliloquy of the fallen cardinal, which in verbal grandeur is second only to the soliloquy of Hamlet. In part it is as follows:

"Farewell, a long farewell to all my greatness!
This is the state of man: to-day he puts forth
The tender leaves of hope; to-morrow blossoms,
And bears his blushing honors thick upon him;
The third day comes a frost, a killing frost,
And, when he thinks, good easy man, full surely
His greatness is a-ripening, nips his root,
And then he falls, as I do."

Then in that last interview with Cromwell, Woolsey advises his friend as follows:

"Cromwell, I charge thee, fling away ambition:
By this sin fell the angels; how can man, then,
The image of his Maker, hope to win by it?"

Green, the historian, says that as Woolsey's end was approaching, he was heard to say to the officer in whose custody he was: "And Master Knighton, had I but served God as diligently as I served the king, He would not have given me over in my gray hairs." Shakespeare places this scene in that last interview with Cromwell, and recites it thus:

" .   .   .   O Cromwell, Cromwell!
Had I but served my God with half the zeal
I served my king, He would not in mine age
Have left me naked to mine enemies."

But Cromwell did not profit by the fallen Woolsey's advice: on the contrary, he climbed the ladder of ambition to a dizzy height, and fell with a crash more cruel than the fall of Woolsey.

Henry VIII. was as nearly an absolute monarch as England ever knew. Under Woolsey, and then under Thomas Cromwell, the power of the people and Parliament disappeared, and Henry's stubborn and cruel will became the law of the land.

Those who wish to hear Henry VIII. soundly berated, I refer to Mr. Dickens, and I feel the utmost confidence that all their pent-up vindictiveness shall be satisfied. Yet strange to say, James Anthony Froude, a popular English historian of the Victorian era, lauded Henry VIII. to the skies. To my mind this only goes to prove that no event in history is so well established but that some writer will dispute it.

This strong, bold, and wicked monster died in the year 1547, after afflicting England thirty-eight years, and he was succeeded by his only son, the child of Jane Seymour, as

EDWARD VI.

This young king was but nine years old when he came to the throne, and throughout his short reign he was wholly under the domination of his maternal uncles, the Seymours, and one of these uncles married Catherine Parr, the widow of the late king. The Seymours quarreled and fought among themselves, as to which uncle should have precedence in the councils of the royal closet. But most that either king or uncles did was to persecute Roman Catholics so cruelly that its reaction fell heavily upon the Protestants in the succeeding reign.

There was an effort made to marry Edward to Mary, Queen of Scots, then a child of ten years, but her friends being Roman Catholics, regarded Edward as a wicked heretic, and nothing came of it; for, according to the dogmatic religion instilled into the mind of this child-queen, heresy was ten times over a greater crime than murder. England went to war with Scotland about it, because of wounded national pride; and a Scottish nobleman being captured by the English, was asked why they objected to the match, and his reply was: "O, no objection, none in the world, to the match, but only your manner of wooing."

In the year 1553, Edward VI. died, at the age of fifteen, and there was an attempt to force the crown on a young lady known in history as the Lady Jane Grey, a Protestant cousin of Edward; but the attempt resulted only in the cruel death of the Lady Jane, and many of her great friends; and the crown was given to Edward's elder sister, the daughter of Catherine of Aragon, who became England's first queen, as

MARY TUDOR.

Mary was England's first female sovereign. She was a Roman Catholic, and her accession greatly retarded the progress of the Reformation. This queen is known in history as *Bloody Mary*, in allusion to her bloody career in persecuting Protestants; but the historian Miles thinks this harsh description is not deserved, for while she did burn a few Protestants to death, and among them that prince of preachers, Hugh Lattimer, the number that suffered under her was much smaller than is generally believed. Besides, that historian thinks these atrocities should be attributed to the times, and not to the queen herself. Anent this reason, one can't help speculating on how reassuring it would be to know that all our crimes would be attributed to the times. Ridpath says that three hundred persons were burned at the stake during the five years of the queen's reign. It would be hard to invent a plausible excuse for such inhuman cruelty, and it is not often a historian attempts it.

Mary married Philip II. of Spain, that king that is on record as never having laughed but once in all his life, and that was when he heard of the massacre of St. Bartholomew. Philip was himself a bigoted Catholic, and a devout believer in the Holy Inquisition, which he attempted to introduce into England; but the frown of the nation was too ominous to be mistaken, and the scheme was abandoned.

It ought to be said to Mary's credit that most of the time during which these three hundred Protestants were roasting, she herself was sick in body and mind, neglected by her husband, and was immured in the strictest seclusion, so it is hardly possible that she personally had knowledge of many of these murders. But that same instrument of torture, the Church, was given a free hand, and that answered quite as well for the purpose.

Mary died childless in the year 1558. Ridpath says:

"Nature had set its edict against the propagation of monsters."

The revolting crimes committed in the name of the Roman Catholic religion, during this reign, badgered England into that intense Protestant nation it has been since the days of Mary Tudor.

During this reign England lost the city of Calais, her last foothold in France; and Mary took this loss so grievously to heart, that she is said to have told her friends that after her death, if her body were opened, the word "*Calais*" would be found burnt into the surface of her heart.

When the news of Mary's death reached Parliament, that august body gave way to the bad taste of indulging in a general buzz of satisfaction, interspersed with suppressed cries of "*Long Live Queen Elizabeth.*"

ELIZABETH.

As we have seen, Elizabeth was the only daughter of Anne Boleyn, the second wife of Henry VIII. This queen was a wonderful woman. It has been said that she *had* no religion, but was forced to espouse the Protestant cause for the obvious reason that the Roman Catholic Church disputed the validity of Henry's divorce from Catherine of Aragon, and as a necessary consequence, disputed the legality of his marriage with Anne Boleyn, which, of course, precluded Elizabeth's legitimacy.

Elizabeth is known in history as the *great queen*, but in many respects she was not great. Mr. Dickens describes her as, "Red-headed, freckle-faced, and much given to hard swearing." I am frank to admit that anything Mr. Dickens said is usually worthy of consideration; for it is probably true that of the myriads of men that lived and died during the thousand years embraced in this story, not one wrought more effectively for the alleviation of human suffering, or added more to the sum total of human happiness, than did Charles Dickens. But as a proof of the fact that the *"dram of eale"* is present with the greatest of mortal men, we here see the great master sneering at the color of a lady's hair! The truth is, with the single exception of gray, that rich, golden color contemptuously called "red" is the most beautiful color of all shades for the hair of a lady. But it is pleasanter to think with Burns' omnamorous lines:

> "There's muckle love in raven locks,
>   The flaxen ne'er grows yoden,
> There's kiss and hause me in the brown,
>   And glory in the goden."

59

But the historian Green comes with a more serious charge and says: "In the profusion and recklessness of her *lies*, Elizabeth stood without a peer in Christendom." Another historian tells us that once when one of her bishops had the hardihood to call on the queen and protest against the injustice of certain "reliefs" she had demanded of the clergy, Elizabeth rose in her majesty and replied: "Proud prelate! You pay in those reliefs, or, by God, I'll unfrock you!" It has well been said, "We can much forgive Elizabeth, the woman, for the sake of Elizabeth, the queen." The true greatness of Queen Elizabeth lay in her superb self-possession, and her ability to take the tide at the flood, and ride the crest of the wave.

It is a matter of common knowledge that human thought moves in *waves;* and in Elizabeth's time this thought-wave attained the proportions of a veritable billow, which, like all thought-waves, crystallized into great men, and intellectual vigor ran riot. It was this reign that produced Shakespeare, who, as a literary genius and depicter of human nature, beggared the past, and bankrupted the future: it was this reign that produced Drake, probably the greatest sea captain of all time; and Sir Francis Bacon, the inventor of our system of inductive philosophy; and Sir Walter Raleigh, universally known as the "Prince of Gentlemen." This reign produced hundreds of men, now unknown, but any one of whom would have come down to us in history as an intellectual giant, but for the immediate presence of greater. Ben Jonson would have been Shakespeare, but for the bard of Stratford-on-Avon.

But it seems to be a universal law,—a protest of nature, as it were,—that all over-rapid growth produces excrescences that mar beauty and symmetry. This is true in the material world, as well as in the mental and spiritual development. There is no more perfect symmetry in all nature than that of the hand of a normal child, but the hand of a rapidly growing boy is often marred with unsightly warts. The brilliant valedictorian too often goes off at a tangent, while sturdy mediocrity marches steadily to the front. Piety is manhood's most glorious ornament, but the zealot is almost sure to bring reproach and ridicule on the worship he adores.

The excrescence produced by the vigor of Elizabethan scholarship was that unnatural affectation of style, known as Euphuism, so named from its foremost disciple, a creation of the fancy, called *Euphues*. A popular writer of the times, named Lyly, wrote a book called "Euphues and His Anatomy of Wit," which gave the name to this style, which might be called, Gallantry gone to seed, courtly manners so stilted as to be ridiculous. Below, I quote a paragraph written by Sir Walter Scott, which he gave as an example of sixteenth century Euphuism:

"Credit me, fairest lady, that such is the cunning of our English courtiers of the hodiernal strain, that as they have infinitely refined upon the plain and rusticial discourse of our fathers, which, as I may say, more beseemed the mouths of country roysterers in a May-game than that of courtly gallants in the galliards; so I hold it ineffably and unutterably impossible that those who may succeed us in that garden of wit and courtesy shall alter or amend it. Venus delighted but in the language of Mercury, Bucephalous will stoop to no one but Alexander, none can sound Apollo's harp but Orpheus."

A Thousand Years With Royalty.

Of course such foolishness as this would disgust the common sense of any people; and in England there was such a revulsion of feeling that Euphuism soon found its antithesis in the blunt and unmusical speech of the Puritans, and the beauties of Shakespeare were sunk in oblivion for nearly two centuries.

We shall see that this vigorous thought-wave was succeeded by a period of depression and stupidity in the next reign, only to revive in a religious wave of tremendous force and vigor, that crystallized in Oliver Cromwell, John Milton, and John Bunyan; but to revert to Elizabeth:

Justice to the great queen demands that one other mark of true greatness be mentioned as possessed by Elizabeth to a degree that not only astonished the world of her day, but has excited the admiration of every generation since. The history of the world has shown that an outraged woman come into power is a dangerous proposition, and almost sure to display vindictive cruelty. With Queen Elizabeth this was not the case. Though her childhood and girlhood was one continuous insult and outrage,—branded as a bastard, disowned by her father, treated as a pariah by her brother Edward, hated and scorned by her sister Mary and all the Catholics of England, and all this time treated as a virtual prisoner by her harsh and unsympathetic guardian, or rather her custodian, Sir Henry Benefield; then to be called directly from all this injustice and insult, to unlimited power, was enough to turn almost any head.

But it has been stated that Elizabeth affected to forget her wrongs, and her revolution was accomplished without the shedding of one drop of blood. Even when Sir Henry Benefield came fawning at the feet of his erstwhile ward, the queen, with dignity, informed him that when she should have some state prisoner that was to be treated with unusual severity, she might call for him as a tormentor; and curtly dismissed him.

Queen Elizabeth never married. She was wont to say that she wedded her kingdom when she was crowned queen of England, and that she would bring no other husband over her people. But the historian Miles spitefully remarks that she did not say this till she was an old woman. It is pleasant to compare this churlish thrust with Shakespeare's gallant allusion, in those delightful lines in "Midsummer Night's Dream," where Oberon is represented as saying to Puck:

> "   .   .   .   Thou rememberest
> Since once I sat upon a promontory
> And heard a mermaid on a dolphin's back
> Uttering such dulcet and harmonious breath
> That the rude sea grew civil at her song.
> And certain stars shot madly from their spheres,
> To hear the sea-maid's music.
>   That very time I saw, but thou couldst not,
> Flying between the cold moon and earth,
> Cupid all armed: A certain aim he took
> At a fair vestal throned by the west,
> And loosed his love-shaft smartly from his bow,
> As it would pierce a hundred thousand hearts;
> But I might see young Cupid's fiery shaft
> Quenched in the chased beams of the watery moon,
> And the imperial voteress passed on,
> In maiden meditation, fancy-free."

Elizabeth reigned forty-five years, and died in the year 1603, and with her the Tudor line ended. Historians differ a little about what Elizabeth did and said about choosing her successor. Dickens says that when the great queen was about to die, she charged her ministers to see that no *rascal's son* filled her place when she was dead, but to see that her successor was the son of a king. And that when the ministers pressed her to *name* her choice, she replied: "Who should be but our cousin of Scotland?" meaning James Stuart, the King of the Scots. But Green says that the ministers asked Elizabeth if she willed that James should be her successor, and that she merely raised her hand to her head, which was interpreted as her assent.

It was thought by the enemies of Elizabeth that remorse for having ordered the execution of James' mother, Mary, Queen of Scots, induced the dying queen to desire Mary's son as her successor, as a sort of restitution. But Elizabeth had, in the course of her long reign, become a sincere Protestant, and James was the nearest Protestant heir to the English throne, he being, as we have seen, a son of Mary, Queen of Scots, and her husband, Lord Darnley, both of whom were grandchildren of Margaret Tudor, who married James IV. of Scotland.

Elizabeth's immense popularity was largely due to the destruction of the Spanish Armada. With that splendid victory for the British navy, patriotism fairly boiled over, and the universal adoration of the queen became a blind and unreasoning worship.

The romantic stories of Queen Elizabeth's lovers are too long for this brief sketch, and I must refer my readers to those intensely interesting love passages as they appear in Elizabethan history. Sir Walter Scott's "Kenilworth" gives an interesting and tragic account of Lord Leicester's aspiration to the queen's hand, and how, for this ambition, the beautiful Amy Robsart was cruelly done to death. The book opens by quoting a touching poem of the olden time, called "Cumner Hall," directly referring to this tragedy. The first stanza is as follows:

"The dews of summer night did fall,
The moon, sweet regent of the sky,
Silvered the walls of Cumner Hall,
And many an oak that grew thereby."

Even now, after the lapse of more than three hundred years, it is rarely, if ever, disputed that England's most illustrious sovereign passed away in the good year 1603.

Queen Elizabeth was succeeded by

JAMES I.

The first sovereign of the ill-starred House of Stuart to sit on the throne of England. He was James VI. of Scotland, and only son of that beautiful, but erratic, queen known in history as Mary, Queen of Scots, whom, in spite of her hideous crimes, "the world has persisted in loving instead of Elizabeth."

The story of James I. and his forbears will be lightly touched on here, for the reason that they properly belong to the story of the Scottish sovereigns, which is supposed to follow this compilation.

James I. has come down to us more as a disgusting joke than as a real king. He was an eminent scholar, and was vainly proud of his learning. A wit of the time referred to him as, "The wisest fool in Christendom." He wrote a number of books, one of the most notable being on the subject of *Witchcraft*, in which he devoutly believed. The Duke of Buckingham, James' court favorite, was in the habit of referring to the king as, *"His Sowship,"* and Dickens thought the title was aptly applied.

This king quarreled with, and cajoled, his parliaments, and was a real master of a certain kind of sarcasm. Once when a parliamentary committee waited on the king to protest against some high-handed act, James received them with an affluence of mock courtesy, and loudly called to an attendant, *"Fetch stools for the Ambassadors!"*

If James I. had been the strong man that Henry VIII. was, he would have been as absolute; but being only a weak coward, he resorted to bribery, and his court became shamelessly venal.

Yet it was under James I. that our authorized translation of the Holy Scriptures was made. The real credit for this is not due to James, however, but rather to the fag-end of the Elizabethan scholars; for James' reign was distinctively the reaction after the vigor of the reign of Elizabeth.

It was under this James that America's first successful colony was planted, and named Jamestown in honor of the king, and a few years later the Pilgrims settled at Plymouth.

Sir Walter Scott's "Fortunes of Nigel" gives us a good insight into the character of James I., and is more merciful to his memory than any history I have seen.

James died, it is said of gluttony, in the year 1625, and was succeeded by his son, "Baby Charles," as he was fondly called by the doting father. A daughter of James I. married the Duke of Brunswick, a fact I mention here to make clear later on the right of the House of Hanover; for it was a daughter of this daughter, who, by the Act of Settlement, seventy years after James' death, was declared the rightful heir to the throne after the failure of the House of Stuart.

CHARLES I.

Charles I. was crowned King of England in 1625. He has often been referred to as "The Blessed Martyr"; but it is not so much the fashion now as it was a century ago, and, as time rolls on, history will doubtless fix him with his proper appellation of *Unspeakable Tyrant*. The historian Green began the study of English History as a boy, with undoubting faith in the old loyalist idea that Charles was indeed a martyr, and that those who were responsible for his death were *more* than murderers, they were murderers of the Lord's Anointed! But as the true character of Charles dawned upon the young student, he completely reversed himself; and regardless of the social ostracism he suffered, he became the author of Green's *History of the English People*, probably the most exact portrayal of England's great past, from the standpoint of the common people, that has ever been written.

The lull of stagnation that followed the vigor of Elizabeth's reign gave place, under Charles I., to another thought-wave, which took the form of religious enthusiasm, and produced Oliver Cromwell, the most powerful personality in all English history. Charles was a tyrant, pure and simple, though, it must be admitted, not a very cruel one; for religious bigotry is the most cruel of all forms of bigotry, and Charles was a personal tyrant. His belief in the Divine Right of Kings was almost sublime. His creed was: "The king can do no wrong: he is God's vice-regent on earth: he is to rule, and the people are to obey without question."

For twenty-four years there was strife between the king and the Parliament, and this strife culminated in civil war, and all this time the religious enthusiasts grew stronger and stronger. And now it was that Oliver Cromwell came forward like a lion rousing from his sleep, and his genius as an organizer soon made him, not only the people's unquestioned leader, but the idol of the nation as well.

In January, 1649, Charles was tried for treason, condemned and executed; but the unfair means adopted to secure his conviction has given his execution the name of murder. There was quite a large party in Parliament that stood aghast at the idea of *regicide*, and the Cromwell party, being in doubt as to how the vote would stand, ordered Colonel Pride, with thirty soldiers, to post himself at the entrance of the House of Commons, with a list of members known to be friendly to the king, and to arrest these members as they came out of the House. This was done; and when a member would ask by what authority the arrest was made, Colonel Pride's laconic answer was: "By the authority of the Sword!" This incident is known in history as "*Pride's Purge.*"

Charles' family fled to the continent, and it was not till the year 1660, after the death of the great Oliver, that his eldest son was recalled. This period, from 1649 to 1660, is known by the English people, as *The Interregnum*, but by all the rest of the world, as *The Days of the Commonwealth;* for the English people, as a nation, have never recognized the Commonwealth, but refer to the year 1660 as the twelfth year of the reign of Charles II., usually written, 12 Car., II.

During the years of the Commonwealth, or the Interregnum, as you may choose to call the period,

OLIVER CROMWELL

Was supreme in England, as the Protector.

Reinforced by that terrible brigade of soldiers known in history as Oliver's Ironsides, no power on earth could withstand him. The Old Guard of Napoleon, and the Tenth Legion of Cæsar have furnished matter for the poet and the orator, till they are on the lips of almost every schoolboy; but, as a fighting machine, Oliver's Ironsides have never been equaled in all the annals of war. They went into battle singing Psalms, and bore down all opposition, no matter what the odds against them. They were never once defeated.

Cromwell did many cruel acts, and his hands were deep dyed in the blood of his country, but he made England more respected and feared abroad than she had been for a century before his time, or a century after. He swept the seas clear of pirates, and "stopped the persecuting fires of Rome."

A Thousand Years With Royalty.

The torrents of abuse that early historians, who wrote from the standpoint of royalty, have heaped upon the head of Cromwell, have caused many well-informed people to regard him as a common, ignorant boor, with no virtue, save brute courage. This is altogether erroneous. Cromwell was of noble family. On his father's side, he was descended from the family of Lord Thomas Cromwell, Prime Minister under Henry VIII., while his mother was a scion of the royal House of Stuart, and a relative of Charles I. He was a member of the Parliament that took up the gage of battle when it was thrown down by Charles, and he was quite able to write letters in the Latin language.

The Cromwell party cropped their hair close, and for this reason were contemptuously called *"Roundheads,"* while the party of the royalists, in the same spirit of derision, were called *"Cavaliers,"* from their pompous military mien. So the fight between the Roundheads and Cavaliers drave on, with steady success to the Roundheads, till the year 1658, when the Protector died, and his party melted away like snow before the sun of springtime.

Before Cromwell died, he designated his son Richard as his successor as Lord Protector; but what is gotten by violence must be maintained by violence, and Richard was altogether unable to cope with the turning tide, and resigned his office within five months; and the army, under General Monk, dictated the policy of the Commonwealth until the recall of the "rightful" king, who had been in banishment since the death of his father in 1649.

Sir Walter Scott's "Woodstock," though written from the viewpoint of a partisan cavalier, gives a vivid picture of the troublous days of the Interregnum. The pride and poverty of old Sir Henry Lee is terribly suggestive to us who have seen his exact prototype in the survivors of our Southern ante-bellum aristocracy. From the standpoint of utility, altogether impracticable, but so really great that there is no dislodgment, but——death.

CHARLES II.

In the year 1660, the eldest son of Charles I. was recalled from banishment, and seated on the throne of the House of Stuart. Puritanism passed with Cromwell and the Commonwealth, and under Charles II. the reaction was sharp and frightful. Profligacy became honorable. Court ladies vied with each other in obscenity; chastity was flouted as the affectation of a prude; female virtue became a reproach, instead of a grace; London, loosed from the trammels of Puritanism, rushed into Sodom and Gomorrah. The king himself led the pace, and he was not wanting in followers.

It was at this time the immortal Milton wrote his "Paradise Lost," and the name he gave the great epic was suggested by the terrible fall of the English people from the religion of the Puritans to the unspeakable profligacy of Charles' court. It was also at this time that John Bunyan, while a prisoner in Bedford jail, for conscience' sake, wrote his "Pilgrim's Progress"; for with all the shameless wickedness of Charles' reign, there were stringent laws against worshipping God except by the ritual of the established Church of England, and for this offence Bunyan was imprisoned. It was this intolerance towards the religion of the Puritans that induced the tremendous emigration from England to America during the reign of Charles II.

Most historians describe Charles II. as a good-natured, easy-going king, with no morals at all, and too indolent to be a menace to the liberties of his people; but Green gives him the character of being able and crafty, only biding his time to become as absolute as his cousin, Louis XIV. of France, whose pensioner he was to the day of his death.

On Charles' recall from banishment, he proclaimed a general amnesty, but he did not respect it; which reminds us of Mr. Dickens' biting sarcasm, when he remarked that the breaking of promises was the distinguishing characteristic of the House of Stuart. Charles persecuted ruthlessly, and even made war on the dead. The bones of the great Cromwell were torn from their resting place, and hanged in chains, by men who did not dare to look into Cromwell's living face.

The Great Plague, followed by the Great Fire of London, are notable events of this reign, and to a certain class of readers their history has a fascination because of the very horror of the scenes; but to most healthy minds the more interesting part of the history of Charles II. is his romantic escape from England after his disastrous defeat at Worcester, in 1651, and this incident is made the climax of Scott's great novel, "Woodstock," referred to above.

In the year 1685 Charles II. died without legitimate issue, and was succeeded by his brother,

JAMES II.

James had enjoyed the titles of Duke of York, and Duke of Albany, and it was for him that our great state and city of New York were named,—as was, also, the city of Albany, the capital of that state.

Of all the bad lot of the House of Stuart, James II. was the worst. He possessed the vices of his race, without any offsetting virtue, and in him despotism developed itself in a form unmitigated by any mildness or weakness of temper. His career was short, but bloody. It was under this king that the infamous Judge Jeffreys flourished, whose very name has become a synonym of judicial ferocity.

Since the reign of Mary Tudor, England had been intensely Protestant, and James II. was a bigoted Roman Catholic. He demanded of his Parliament that the Test Act be repealed, and on its being refused, he *dispensed* with the law. He defiantly set aside the ancient constitutions of England, and refused to be advised to moderation, even by the Pope of Rome. In the year 1688 matters arrived at such a pass that the English people rose in their might and expelled James from the throne, and called his daughter Mary, with her husband, William Henry, Prince of Orange, Stadtholder of Holland, jointly to reign over England; while James fled to the court of Louis XIV. of France, and for a number of years made war on England from that base. This war was virtually closed by James' defeat at the battle of Boyne.

A cruel despot and religious tyrant, his private life was such as we expect of a man with no religious restraint of any kind. Yet attempts have been made to excuse his vile conduct by comparing him with David of Old, as being indeed a great sinner, but also a great repenter. But

Macaulay has pointed out that as often as he repented, he forthwith repented of his repentance. After shamelessly neglecting his queen and spending days together with his mistress, he would go to the queen in deep contrition, and in her presence beat himself over the shoulders with a stick till the blood ran down to the ground; then the very next week he would sneak back, like a dog returning to his vomit.

When James was fleeing from England, alarmed at the wrath of his subjects, he was captured on the Kentish coast by some poor fishermen, who knew only from his skulking demeanor that he was some refugee, and they presuming him to be a culprit, fleeing from justice, treated him rather harshly. In answer to his imperative demands that they release him, the fishermen called him "hatchet face." This was an insult that he never forgave. In after years, when he, waiting at Saint Germain for a reaction to restore him to the throne, would, at times of deep religious fervor, state to his attendants that he had made up his mind to forgive all his enemies, except those fishermen that called him "hatchet face." But the expected reaction never came, and in the year 1701 James died at Saint Germain in France.

The joint sovereigns that succeeded James II. were

WILLIAM AND MARY

The name of this joint reign is preserved familiarly to us in the name of an honored seat of learning in our State of Virginia. Mary died of smallpox in the year 1694, and the love of her people was shown by an affluence of sorrow seldom exhibited by the English nation.

After Mary's death, her husband reigned alone, as

WILLIAM III.

The reign of William and Mary, and that of William III., taken together, form the period of the House of Nassau, and is a break in the Stuart line.

During the reign of William III., in a time of great financial distress, a Scotchman named William Patterson came forward with the first idea of the Bank of England; and from this beginning the colossal banking business of the world has grown. It was also in this reign that the House of Commons gained the ascendency which it has held with ever-increasing power and authority to the present day.

William III. was probably the greatest statesman, and assuredly the greatest diplomat, that ever sat on the throne of England; but his best energies were sadly distracted from home affairs by his almost constant wars with France.

There were no children of William and Mary's marriage, and as the children of the Princess Anne, Mary's sister (and, by the way, Anne was the mother of eighteen children), all died in childhood, and Anne being the heir apparent to the throne, the question of the succession became all-important; so there was passed an Act of Parliament, known in history as the Act of Settlement, by the terms of which the succession was fixed, after Anne, on the Electress Sophia of Hanover, and her heirs "*being Protestant*"; for the Electress, as we have seen, was the granddaughter of King James I.

William III. died in the year 1702, and the crown passed, by the terms of the Act of Settlement, to Mary's sister,

75

ANNE.

This queen was of rather feeble intellect, and her husband, Prince George, brother of the King of Denmark, was an insufferable dolt. He was nicknamed *"Est il Possible,"* from the fact that this was his invariable exclamation at everything said in his presence, no matter how commonplace. William always had the greatest contempt for him, and he is quoted by Macaulay as saying: "I have tried Prince George drunk, and I have tried him sober, and there is nothing in him."

But for all that, Anne's reign was a glorious one for England. The Duke of Marlboro was the queen's advisor, and he was both a great statesman, and a great general. Under his administration the French were whipped off the seas, and beaten at every turn on land; and England rose to the rank of *first* among European States.

It was during this, and the first decade of the succeeding reign, that Rev. Isaac Watts, the sweetest singer of devotional melody since Hebrew David, composed and published the beautiful and inspiring hymns that we sing in our churches to this day.

Anne is the last sovereign in England that has presumed to veto an Act of Parliament; that ancient prerogative of the crown was absorbed by the ever-increasing majesty of the people; and in this particular the sovereign of Great Britain is less powerful than the president of the United States.

Under Queen Anne the watchword of English trade was *Thrift,* and the American colonies grew and prospered; and on her death, in the year 1714, the verdict of the world was that she had made a great queen, and that her reign had been a blessing to the English race. Anne was the last of the House of Stuart.

The Electress Sophia having died in the year 1713, her eldest son, George Louis, then a man fifty-four years of age, was called to the throne of England as

GEORGE I.

This king was the first of the House of Hanover, and this royal house holds the sceptre of England to the present day.

This George was a German in all his tastes and sympathies. His preference for all things German placed a great gulf between him and his subjects, and their antipathy was mutual. Other things contributed to make George I. a failure as an English king: twenty years before his accession to the English throne, his duchess was caught in a love intrigue, and divorced, and from that day to the day of her death, more than thirty years, she was a virtual prisoner; for the duchess, on being overtaken in her fault, and seeing her lover slain, boldly asserted that her husband frittered away *his* time with his mistresses, and that the time would come when that code of morals which assumed that conjugal infidelity was the privilege of the male sex alone would be exploded.

This bold stand did not inure to the personal benefit of the duchess at the time, but it raised a point that has kept people thinking to the present day. And just between you and me, there have been great moral reforms in the history of the world that were slower a-growing than this doctrine preached by poor, disgraced Sophia Dorothea.

77

This scandal hung about the neck of the king, probably with more sinister effect than if *he* had been the disgraced party; for his brutal harshness to the fallen duchess was resented in the king, though those who resented it were as far from forgiving the poor lady as the king himself was. Strange inconsistency; but we are all that way. Then the disgraceful quarrel between the king and his son, the Prince of Wales, gave great scandal to the court and embittered George's life.

George I. died in the year 1727, just a year after the death of the imprisoned duchess, while on a visit to his native land, of which he was also the nominal ruler.

This George has been compared with William III., in that both were foreigners, and each called from his foreign possession to rule over England; but the historian that makes this comparison admits that it is comparing an intellectually great man with an intellectually small one; which admission quite robs George I. of what would otherwise be a high compliment.

George I. was quietly succeeded by his son, George Augustus, known as

GEORGE II.

Ridpath says that George II. was like his father in his detestation of all things English, but was possessed of less ability than George I. The reign of George II. would have come down to us without a feature to redeem it from infamy had not his queen, Wilhelmena Caroline, fondly remembered as "Caroline the Beloved," shed a glory about the court of this king, that has done much to dispel the gloom created by her mean-spirited lord, for,—

"As unto the bow the cord is,
So unto the man is woman."

It was this good, kind queen that is represented as coming to the assistance of *Jeannie Deans*, in Scott's admirable novel, "The Heart of Midlothian."

During this reign the Jacobites, the supporters of the Catholic descendants of James II., as against the House of Hanover, gave the government much trouble, and in the year 1745, Charles Edward, a grandson of James, landed in Scotland, and the Highlanders rose and flocked to his standard in great numbers. He gained considerable headway at first; but in 1746, he was defeated in the famous battle of Culloden by the Duke of Cumberland, the king's brother, and Charles Edward made his escape by aid of the celebrated Flora McDonald.

Charles Edward is known in history as the *Young Pretender;* and he is the "Charlie" referred to in the old Jacobite songs that we, who are of Scotch descent, had sung to us in childhood by our grandmothers, notably:

"Over the water, over the sea,
Over the water to Charlie;
Charlie loves good ale and wine,
Charlie loves good brandy,
Charlie loves a pretty girl,
As sweet as sugar-candy."

It is true, this old song was made and published by the ultra Cavaliers during the banishment of Charles II., but it never came into popularity till it was used as a Jacobite song as referring to the Young Pretender. Mr. Dickens said that of all the history and influence of the House of Stuart, there is nothing left to posterity so delightful as these old Jacobite songs.

79

Under King George II., England was fortunate in having at the head of affairs Sir Robert Walpole as Prime Minister, a statesman of great ability, and who was equal to the task of steering the Ship of State clear of the multitude of dangerous breakers, into which the king's wilful disregard of duty constantly threatened to drive her. But historians credit Queen Caroline with influencing the king to retain this great minister.

George II. was harsh and unfatherly to his son, Frederick, the Prince of Wales, as if *he* had not seen the evil of this unnatural family strife in his own youth. And Ridpath says that even Caroline was unkind to Frederick; but this is so out of joint with Caroline's character and nature, I choose to believe this seeming dislike was assumed, to appease the king's ungovernable temper.

It was during this reign that our great state of Georgia was colonized, and named in honor of the king. It was also in this reign that the English courts of law discarded the Latin language for English,—a decided gain, both in nationality and common sense.

Frederick, the Prince of Wales,—that prince for whom the city of Fredericksburg, Va., and Frederick, Md., were named, died before his father did. So when George II. died in the year 1760, the son of Frederick, a grandson of George II., succeeded to the throne, as

GEORGE III.

This obstinate king has been held up to the world as a man not to be swerved from duty by any sort of consideration.   But George III. did England more harm than Henry VIII.; more harm than Mary Tudor, or James II. His foolish obstinacy lost to England the American colonies. His mother was a strong-minded, ambitious woman, who was disappointed herself of being Queen of England, and the whole of her enormous power over her son was exerted to assist him to thwart the will of the people.   As the king dismissed adviser after adviser and minister after minister, his mother would exult, and exclaim with great satisfaction, "Now, indeed, is my son a king!"

There were stirring times in this reign, and many important events occurred, among them the American Revolution, the French Revolution, the rise, spectacular career, and fall of Napoleon Bonaparte;   and the period was peculiarly fecund of great statesmen, great generals, and great churchmen.   Pitt, Fox, Lord North, Nelson, Wellington, were products of this reign, as was also, John Wesley, whose life work is sufficient to impart lustre to any age.

In a quite different class, one other man lived during this reign, whose name is as nearly immortal as the world has produced in modern times.   I refer to the Scottish bard, Robert Burns.   The statesmanship of Pitt, Fox, and North was fitted only for the times;   the heroism of Nelson and Wellington was great only because it was successful;   and all these will be outshone by greater successes in the future. But Burns' music is absolutely inimitable, and will rouse the souls of men as long as there is a human heart in Caledonia, or blood in the veins of a descendant of one, the world over.   The Scotchman that does not love Burns is not to be trusted.

A Thousand Years With Royalty.

No real history of any man or event can be written till at least one century has elapsed after the event to be written of, for the reason that all men are partisans, whether they themselves know it or not. We Americans regard the War of the Revolution as the greatest event of the age. It was great, for with the pangs of that struggle was born a mighty nation. But common modesty suggests that we pause to remember that during that great war, we had more hearty sympathizers in England than we had enemies in America, and that impartial history will doubtless note the fact.

The true historian is not permitted to dream of the future; but this story is not a history proper, and I claim the freedom of prediction, and the indulgence of sentiment; and in the exercise of that freedom, I pause to predict that the future historian writing a thousand years hence will record something like this:

"The last four decades of the eighteenth century was covered by the foolish and obstinate reign of the third George of the Hanoverian dynasty, who 'lingered superfluous on the stage' till the year 1820; but the latter half of this reign was a virtual regency, for the king was hopelessly demented.

"But there were great and lasting deeds belonging to this reign, independent of the king, and often in his despite, that have preserved the period from oblivion. It was at this time that the poet Burns wrote 'Tam O'Shanter': it was at this time that Bishop Heber wrote that immortal evangelizing hymn, 'From Greenland's Icy Mountains': it was during this reign that the English colonies in America revolted from the senseless tyranny of the king, and by an act of federation formed a republic known as The United States of America, which as the cradle of liberty drew the oppressed of all nations unto it. From the first this republic enjoyed phenomenal prosperity; though its progress was hindered for a time by a class of criminals who ridiculously styled themselves the 'American Aristocracy of Wealth.' This American republic, after repudiating a few anarchists parading in the garb of Socialists, became the leader in that Socialistic propaganda that has permeated the whole world, and brought such sweet harmony out of the jarring discord of former times."

George III. died in the year 1820, after a reign of sixty years, and was succeeded by his son, George Augustus Frederick, as

GEORGE IV.

As stated above these recent sovereigns can have no real history, and it is doubtful if I should add interest to my story by dwelling upon the events of their reigns, hence it is only to fill in the list of kings that I give them brief mention here. Besides, if I were to follow the time-honored maxim, "Speak fair, young master, or speak not at all," I should be obliged to utter the name of George IV. in a whisper; for even the Encyclopedia Britannica can not find in its great English heart a single good thing to say about this king, except that in his youth he was very handsome in person.

This George came to the throne at the age of fifty-eight, a worn-out debauchee, but he had been regent for nine years prior to his father's death. A nauseating scandal between George and his wife had thoroughly disgusted the English people, and on his accession as king, the country was in the humor to strip the sovereign of every vestige of power that had been gained by the stubborn rule of George III., and the ten years of George IV.'s reign sufficed for that purpose.

This reign covered the third decade of the nineteenth century, the palmiest days of Sir Walter Scott; and Mr. Scott was master of ceremonies at a reception given the king by the city of Edinburgh when George visited the ancient capital of Scotland.

As sorry a figure as George IV. made as an English king, there were some really great reforms during his short reign. Prominent among them was the removal of the legal disabilities of Roman Catholics, by which they had been unjustly burdened since the reign of Charles II., as was also Sir Robert Peele's revisal and "humanizing" of the criminal code. Up to this time, there were so many capital offences in the criminal code, which the English nation, out of inordinate conservatism, had from time out of mind refused to amend, the judges had come, from sheer necessity, to commute the sentences of four-fifth of all the criminals convicted in the courts.

During this reign England acquired large additions of territory in the Far East by the conquest of Burmah; and this reign marks that point in English history at which the personality of the crowned head ceased to be a controlling factor in the affairs of Great Britain.

In the year 1830, George IV. died without legitimate issue, and his eldest living brother, William, Duke of Clarence, was crowned King of England, with the title of

WILLIAM IV.

This king was bred to the sea, he being a younger son, and with only remote prospects of ever coming to be England's sovereign; but death made path for his promotion, little expected by William, or by the English people. William IV. was a soldier of considerable ability, but he was altogether wanting in "kingcraft."

As Queen Anne was the last sovereign to exercise the prerogative of the veto, so William IV. was the last to attempt to impose an unpopular ministry on the English people. But he had the wit to coerce an obstreperous House of Lords, by the threat to "create" new lords enough to form a majority. The king's order for this expedient is still considered as the first effective thrust that was to destroy the *rotten borough* system of the English Parliament. It is a short order, and I give it in full:

"The king grants permission to Earl Gray, and his Chancellor, Lord Brougham, to create such a number of peers as will be sufficient to insure the passing of the Reform Bill, first calling up Peers' eldest sons.—William R.

Windsor Castle, May 17th, 1832."

The lords promptly passed the Reform Bill without the aid of the new peers; and many lawmakers believe to this day that no more salutary law was ever enacted by the English Parliament.

William IV. died in the year 1837, and was succeeded by his niece, the Princess Alexandria Victoria, daughter of Edward, Duke of Kent, who was the fourth son of George

III.; for a strange fatality seems to have overtaken the male heirs of the House of Hanover, much like the failure of the male Tudor line after Henry VIII. The plain truth is, the curse of God had fallen on the male line of both these royal houses, because of their notorious contempt for conjugal fidelity.

A happy era dawned for England the day the successor of William IV. was crowned queen, as

VICTORIA.

This great and good queen reigned sixty-four years, the longest reign in all English history, and, I believe, the most beneficent for the human race. Her long reign was an era of invention, and nearly all the phenomena of nature were solved by man. The application of steam as a motive power: the lightning of the sky harnessed and made to obey the will of man: the manufacture and use of the high explosives, brought into the reach of man powers and forces undreamed of before in the history of the world. All these, and many others, were the discoveries of the Victorian reign.

This queen began her reign at the age of eighteen, and at the time of her death in 1901, she was eighty-two years old.

Victoria married her cousin, Prince Albert of Saxe-Coburg, whose full name was Francis Charles Augustus Albert Emmanuel, and of this union there were born fifteen children, though a number of them died in infancy.

Prince Albert was distinctively a man of practical affairs, and the conception of the idea of International

Expositions is due to his practical mind. Doubtless history will accord this prince a high place among the benefactors of England; but at this date, it is true he is better known by the name of our regulation dress-coat, than by any of the great things he did for England. Prince Albert died of typhoid fever in 1861, the queen surviving him just forty years.

Upon the death of Victoria, in 1901, her son, the Prince of Wales, succeeded her as

EDWARD VII.

To quote the historian Ridpath, "We have now arrived at a point where perspective ceases for want of distance." The acts and character of this sovereign are too well remembered to require a single line in this story. The events of his nine years' reign are as the daily news read in the morning papers.

Edward VII. died in 1910, and was succeeded by his son, as

GEORGE V.

This king is the present sovereign of Great Britain.

Since the accession of the House of Hanover the kingly office in England had become merely titular. The House of Commons having forged to the front in the days of William III., has never lost its prestige, but, on the contrary, it has steadily gained in ascendency and grown in stability, till now, that branch of the government names the Prime Minister, who is the real ruler of the English nation.

Once when Gladstone was Victoria's prime minister, he presented a bill for the queen's signature, which was not to her liking, and she refused her assent. The old minister argued the point with the queen, and explained the benefits that were expected to accrue to the people from the bill; but failing to convince her, he quietly informed her that she *must* sign it. The independence of the queen was offended at the word "must," and she with queenly dignity informed Mr. Gladstone that he was addressing the *Queen of England.* The minister assented and informed her that *he* was the *English People.* That was enough: the bill received the queen's signature.

With the exception of a part of the reign of George III., whose obstinate folly, coupled with a sycophant ministry, lost to England the rich American colonies, the will of the English people has not been seriously resisted by any sovereign of the House of Hanover. Under the wise rule of the House of Commons the government of Great Britain has withstood shock after shock without a tremor in the body politic. Wave after wave broke over her rock-ribbed sides during the years of the Napoleonic wars; and much of the time nearly all Europe, as well as young America, was in league against her; but Great Britain remains to-day easily the First World Power.

Having completed my story, I can not do better than to close with the pregnant lines of Ridpath, the historian:

A Thousand Years With Royalty.

"England abides. The Island-built empire is unshaken
by the storm."

> "'The lion has laid his magnificent head
> Between his paws; but he is not dead!
> The Ocean of Atlas rolls and swells,
> The tide is high and the sea-god sprawls
> Against the wave-worn chalky walls,
> The sailors have made the anchors fast,
> The crooked flukes are under the sea,
> The moving deep 'neath billowy blasts
> That tosses the sea-mew, surges past—
> Britannia, what cares she?
> The poet's dust with the dust of the king
>   Is shrined in the Abbey wall,
> And the Church of Elizabeth spreads her wing
> Above the dome, while the singers sing,
>   In the famous Chapel of Paul."

CHRONOLOGICAL INDEX

CHRONOLOGICAL INDEX

CHRONOLOGICAL INDEX—Continued

www.ingramcontent.com/pod-product-compliance
Lightning Source LLC
Chambersburg PA
CBHW031522270326
41930CB00006B/486